W9-BEJ-975

Study Guide and Workbook

For Myers & Hansen's

EXPERIMENTAL PSYCHOLOGY
FIFTH EDITION

Christine H. Hansen
Oakland University

WADSWORTH
★
™
THOMSON LEARNING

Australia • Canada • Mexico • Singapore • Spain • United Kingdom • United States

Sponsoring Editor: *Vicki Knight*
Assistant Editor: *Jennifer Wilkinson*
Editorial Assistant: *Dan Moneypenny*
Production Editor: *Scott Brearton*
Cover Design: *Laurie Albrecht*
Print Buyer: *Micky Lawler*
Cover Printing: *Webcom*
Printing and Binding: *Webcom*

COPYRIGHT © 2002 the Wadsworth Group. Wadsworth is an imprint of the Wadsworth Group, a division of Thomson Learning, Inc. Thomson Learning™ is a trademark used herein under license.

For more information about this or any other Wadsworth products, contact:
WADSWORTH
511 Forest Lodge Road
Pacific Grove, CA 93950 USA
www.wadsworth.com
1-800-423-0563 (Thomson Learning Academic Resource Center)

All rights reserved. No part of this work may be reproduced, transcribed or used in any form or by any means—graphic, electronic, or mechanical, including photocopying, recording, taping, Web distribution, or information storage and/or retrieval systems—without the prior written permission of the publisher.

For permission to use material from this work, contact us by
www.thomsonrights.com
fax: 1-800-730-2215
phone: 1-800-730-2214

Printed in Canada
10 9 8 7 6 5 4 3 2 1

ISBN: 0-534-56009-1

*This workbook is dedicated to my students: past, present,
and future psychological scientists*

STUDY GUIDE AND WORKBOOK CONTENTS

TO THE STUDENT

What will you learn?

You have purchased the workbook and study guide to accompany the fifth edition of *EXPERIMENTAL PSYCHOLOGY*. Each new edition of the textbook has been written with empathy for the seemingly dauntless task confronting students being exposed for the first time to psychological research methods. You will discover that your textbook is very comprehensive, but, also, it is as user-friendly as we could possibly make it. Anne and I have never forgotten how it felt to step into the frightening world of experimental psychology for the first time. We knew we would have to learn a whole new language and master difficult concepts, but we were unprepared for the impact that this course would have on the rest of our lives. No one told us that we would also learn to become more critical and skeptical thinkers--skills we would carry with us the rest of our lives. And, just as important, no one ever told us how much fun research could be once we got the basics behind us!

How hard will it be?

Most students of psychology and related disciplines who take a course in experimental research methods bring with them a sense of dread. It would be untruthful to say that learning research methods is easy--it is not. But, in fact, learning to design and understand psychological research is no more difficult than many of the other courses you will be taking as you progress toward your degree, and a good deal less difficult than some! You can expect, however, that you will need to spend significantly more time learning the material in this course than you do in other psychology and social science courses. For most students, learning about human behavior is intrinsically interesting. That is why so many students with different majors take a course or two in psychology. For the first time, however, you will be learning the *scientific side* of psychology. Furthermore, before you can become proficient in designing and conducting research, you will be faced with the task of putting all your years of experience as a *commonsense psychologist* behind you. Up front, in Chapter 1, we will explain how our intuitive ideas about how things work are frequently incorrect and can actually work against producing good research.

You will also learn that we never actually *prove* anything when we conduct psychological research--even if our research is well-designed. If you have already had a course in statistics, this will not come as a surprise to you. If you have not, you will be very surprised indeed when you learn that research, even experimentation, allows us to accumulate support for our ideas (called *hypotheses*) about the causes of behavior, and the more well-designed the research is, the more confident we can be that we are correct. But the scientific methods for testing our hypotheses allow us only to make probabilistic statements about cause and effect. Good research allows us to say that X is a likely cause of Y, but we can never be completely certain. Take heart in knowing that this problem is one faced by researchers in every scientific discipline who rely on statistics to measure the effects of one variable on another. Good research allows us to explain, and even predict, human behavior with a surprising degree of accuracy. Given the complexity of human beings and human behavior, the fact that we can explain and predict their behavior at all is rather astounding!

Will the workbook and study guide help?

The answer to this question is an unequivocal "Yes!" The authors of your textbook believe that learning research methods lies somewhere between learning a foreign language and learning algebra--and the best technique for learning in these areas is relatively simple: *practice, practice, and more practice.* (Try thinking about it this way: You'll need to learn some definitions represented by a small number of Greek letters, but you won't have to master a new grammatical and pronunciation system at the same time!) Is it worth going to all the trouble of answering the questions and performing the exercises that accompany each textbook chapter? If you want a better grade in the course, my answer is a strong "Yes." For those of you who really want to understand psychological research or are contemplating graduate school, my answer is an even stronger "Yes." The more proficient you can become now, the easier it will be later.

How should you use the workbook and study guide?

Here are a few suggestions. Read the textbook chapter and take notes (or outline the chapter) before you look at the workbook. Incidentally, a number of psychologists now believe that writing it down will improve memory for information because writing adds an additional dimension of memory for the physical actions that accompany the learning (this kind of memory is called "motor memory"), improving our long-term recall of words and images. Go through the workbook pages in order; don't skip around. The order is designed to maximize learning.

The <u>Chapter Outline</u> is placed first to *trigger* your memory for the entire chapter (so don't skip over it). <u>Key Concepts</u> are designed to test your recall of the chapter's *main ideas.* The <u>Key Terms</u> are the important definitions that pertain to the chapter's main ideas. If you are able to define them using (mostly) your own words, you are much more likely to understand what they really mean! Keep your textbook close by. When you get stuck, go back to the appropriate page in the book and reread it until you can answer the question. (The page numbers for looking up the answers are in parentheses next to the questions.) Copying the answer from the book is better than nothing, but it is not as good as actually learning it.

Next do the Fill-In items. They are an additional test of recall--but they test more specific details. The first time through, if you don't know the answer, leave the item blank. The answers are at the end of the chapter, but don't just fill it in with the correct word. Look it up in the book, read the section it comes from, and then fill it in. Read the completed sentence a couple of times until you are sure you have learned the item.

Next, answer the Multiple Choice questions. In general, recognizing an answer is much easier than recalling it, but these questions can seem more difficult because (like the Key Concepts) they require you to remember larger chunks of information, finding the information that fits together as well as the information that does not. Students often ask me whether they should change their answers on multiple choice questions. My answer to that question is, generally, "No"--unless some later test items have triggered new information and you are absolutely sure the new choice is correct and the old one is not. The way we believe memory works, your first choice has a higher likelihood of being correct.

An additional word to the wise: Do not read too much into multiple choice questions. Students who do poorly on multiple choice questions often read things into them. They think about all the things the instructor could have meant and answer a much more difficult question than the instructor had in mind. Remember that when your instructor selected the test questions, each question seemed clear and unambiguous and had only one meaning--the most apparent one.

Next, answer the Short Essay questions. These test your recall of relatively brief, but important, sections within the chapter. At this point, you should be able to answer these without going back to your textbook. If you cannot (or if you are not sure your answer is correct), go back and read the section(s) again. When you are using the workbook, do not attempt to complete an entire chapter in one sitting. At the very least, take a short break after each section. Better yet, distribute studying and self-tests over a period of several days. (Remember the classic research from your introductory psychology class demonstrating that massed practice was *much less efficient* than distributed practice?)

Exercises and Applications and Research are supplementary activities, and your instructor may wish to assign these as homework, class projects, or extra credit. They are designed to give you the opportunity to apply your knowledge and to improve your research skills. If your instructor assigns some of these projects, you will find that they are a lot of fun to complete. And, they are a good way to see, first hand, what it is like to be a psychological scientist.

Christine Hansen

I hope this workbook and study guide makes your task of learning experimental methods and research design easier, and I would appreciate receiving your comments. Simply fill out the card included at the end of the book or send me an e-mail message: chhansen@oakland.edu

MOOSE   Samson

1 PART ONE

INTRODUCTION

This book is divided into four major sections, or parts, which parallel the sections of a research report: *Introduction, Method, Results, and Discussion.* Part 1, the *Introduction*, contains five chapters designed to give you the background you need to understand the scientific method and to begin the process of psychological research.

There are many research designs that can be used to answer psychological questions, but only one, the true experiment, can be used to make causal inferences about behavior. Therefore, techniques of experimentation are the major focus of the book. Very often, however, the questions asked about human behavior cannot--or sometimes should not--be investigated experimentally. At these times, psychological researchers have a wealth of other research methods at their disposal. These methods include nonexperimental and quasi-experimental designs. Each design has strengths and weaknesses, and each presents particular challenges to the researcher.

By the time you have finished Part 1, you should understand (a) why the scientific method is preferable to other ways of knowing, (b) what scientific research methods are available to answer psychological questions, (c) the strengths and weaknesses of each different method, (d) how to come up with a testable hypothesis, (e) how to gather research articles as background for new research, and (f) how to begin writing the *Introduction* to a research report. The first five chapters will take you through these steps.

Chapter 1: Experimental Psychology and the Scientific Method
Chapter 2: Research Ethics
Chapter 3: Alternatives to Experimentation: Nonexperimental Designs
Chapter 4: Alternatives to Experimentation: Correlational and Quasi-Experimental Designs
Chapter 5: Formulating the Hypothesis

1 CHAPTER ONE
Experimental Psychology and the Scientific Method

Chapter Outline (Page numbers refer to textbook pages.)

✓✓ CHAPTER OBJECTIVES: KEY CONCEPTS

Listed below are questions that test the major concepts you should know from Chapter 1. After reading the chapter, you should be able to answer each of the questions below. If not, go back to the book and read the appropriate sections again before continuing on in the Study Guide.

---

1. Why does the psychological researcher need <u>scientific methodology</u>? (4)

2. Describe what is meant by the term <u>nonscientific sources of data</u> and give examples. (5)

3. Explain what <u>nonscientific inference</u> is and give examples. (7)

4. Describe each of the seven <u>characteristics of modern science</u> (scientific mentality, empirical data gathering, seeking general principles, good thinking, self-correction, publicizing results, and replication). (9)

5. Explain the three <u>tools of psychological science</u>: observation, measurement, and experimentation. (15)

6. In scientific terms, what is meant by <u>scientific explanation</u>? (19)

7. What happens in a <u>psychology experiment</u>? (19)

8. How do we explain <u>cause and effect</u> in an experiment? (20)

9. What are the differences between <u>necessary and sufficient causes</u>? (21)

√ QUESTIONS FOR REVIEW AND STUDY

KEY TERMS: *define each term using your own words*

Science (3):

Methodology (3):

Data (3):

Commonsense psychology (4):

Laws (10):

Theory (11):

Good thinking (11):

Parsimony (11):

Falsification (13):

Replication (14):

Observation (15):

Measurement (17):

Experimentation (18):

Testable (18):

Antecedent conditions (19):

Subject (19):

Treatment (19):

Psychology experiment (19):

Cause and effect relationship (20):

√ QUESTIONS FOR REVIEW AND STUDY

FILL INS: *fill in the blanks with the right word or phrase*

1. The _____ of science is what we know, such as the facts we learn in our psychology or chemistry courses.

2. But, science is also a _____ , an activity that includes systematic data gathering, noting relationships, and offering explanations.

3. Commonsense psychology is a form of _____ data gathering.

4. Commonsense psychologists are _____ theorists.

5. Inferring that a woman is serious and unattractive because she is a librarian is called _____ .

6. Feeling more correct about our predictions than we actually are is part of the _____ bias.

7. Alfred North Whitehead postulated that _____ _____ is essential to science.

8. Aristotle set about to describe the existence of order in the universe by collecting _____ data.

9. Explanatory principles that apply to all situations are called _____ ; principles explaining many, but not all, instances of behavior are called _____ .

10. Occam's razor is another term for the principle of _____.

11. The key to studying events that go on inside the person is defining them in terms of events that can be _____.

12. Within the framework of science, observations must be made _____.

13. The same unit of _____ needs to be used each time you measure your observations.

14. Sometimes experimentation is possible, but it cannot be carried out for _____ reasons.

15. The circumstances that come before the event or behavior we wish to explain are called _____.

16. A psychology experiment must compare at least _____ (how many) different treatment conditions.

17. In a psychology experiment, we want to ensure that people who receive one kind of treatment are _____ to people receiving a different treatment.

18. The type of cause and effect relationship established through experiments is called a _____ relationship.

19. The cause and effect relationships established through scientific research commonly involve identifying _____ , rather than necessary, conditions.

Correct answers are located at the end of the chapter, but do not look at them until you have completed the test.

MULTIPLE CHOICE: *circle the best answer to each question*

---

1. The word *science* comes from the Latin word *scientia*, which means _____.
   a. process
   b. content
   c. knowledge
   d. data

2. Which of the following is not a source of commonsense data gathering?
   a. our own observations
   b. our own experiences
   c. learning from others
   d. ESP

3. Deciding that Jerry fell down the stairs because he is a clumsy person (rather than acknowledging that the stairs may have been slippery) is an example of a(n) _____.
   a. situational explanation
   b. trait explanation
   c. stereotype
   d. confirmatory bias

4. Scanlon and her colleagues found evidence that Friday the 13th might be unlucky. What differences did they actually find between Friday the 13th and Friday the 6th?
   a. More cars were driven on Friday the 13th.
   b. More accident victims were treated in emergency rooms on Friday the 13th.
   c. Drivers were found to be more anxious and accident-prone on Friday the 13th.
   d. Drivers who were more cautious got into fewer accidents on Friday the 13th.

5. A European's belief that Americans are violent is a form of _____.
   a. overconfidence bias
   b. stereotyping
   c. trait explanation
   d. parsimony

6. The chances of getting either a head or a tail on any single flip of a coin are 50% (or 1/2). What are the chances of getting three heads in a row?
   a. 1/8
   b. 1/16
   c. 1/32
   d. 1/64

7. The psychologist's goal of prediction is based on the assumption that _____.
   a. behavior follows a natural order
   b. faith is essential to science
   c. people behave in simple ways
   d. if it feels correct it probably is

8. Which of the following is not one of the characteristics of modern science?
   a. scientific mentality
   b. empirical data gathering
   c. self-correction
   d. cross-situational consistency

9. Schlegel argued that what we observe is very much determined by our theory. To offset this, researchers need to employ _____.
   a. good thinking
   b. commonsense psychology
   c. self-correction
   d. trustworthy sources

10. The argument that theories can best be tested through falsification was advanced by _____.
    a. Popper
    b. Whitehead
    c. Aristotle
    d. William of Occam

11. One reason that it is important to communicate research findings by publishing results in scientific journals is that _____.
    a. to keep one's job, a researcher must "publish or perish"
    b. duplicating the failures of others is wasted effort
    c. good scientists work in isolation
    d. scientists can attend professional conferences to exchange information

12. When asked by Mike's friends, his 3-year-old daughter, Abby, seemed to be able to read a children's book called "Where the Wild Things Are." When one of these friends asked Abby to read "Winnie the Pooh," however, Abby could not read a single word. This example illustrates a violation of a characteristic of the scientific method called _____.
    a. good thinking
    b. parsimony
    c. data gathering
    d. replication

13. Only events that are _____ can be studied scientifically.
    a. observable
    b. objective
    c. systematic
    d. falsifiable

14. Which of the following is <u>not</u> one of the tools of psychological science?
    a. observation
    b. measurement
    c. experience
    d. experimentation

15. The specific set of antecedents we create in an experiment are called _____.
    a. explanations
    b. causes
    c. treatments
    d. XYZ

16. For experiments to produce valid conclusions, all explanations except the one(s) being tested should be clearly ruled out. This is known as the principle of _____ .
    a. control
    b. parsimony
    c. observation
    d. falsifiability

Correct answers are located at the end of the chapter, but do not look at them until you have completed the test.

√ QUESTIONS FOR REVIEW AND STUDY

SHORT ESSAY: use the information in the chapter to answer the following questions

1. Discuss the ways in which commonsense psychology can reduce objectivity when we gather data and predict events.

2. What did Whitehead mean by the idea that faith in an organized universe was essential to science? Use an example to help explain your answer.

3. Remember Mike and his daughter, Abby? Mike explained away Abby's failure to read "Winnie the Pooh" by saying that Abby <u>can</u> read-- unless the book is too hard for her.   And, in fact, every time Abby cannot read a book to his friends, he explains that the book must be too hard. (a) Explain why Mike's hypothesis cannot be *falsified*.   (b) Generate a more objective (and also more parsimonious) hypothesis of your own to explain why Abby is able to read only "Where the Wild Things Are."

4. Explain how researchers can investigate mental events. Use an example to illustrate what you mean.

5. How does a psychology experiment demonstrate a cause and effect relationship between antecedent conditions and behavior?

6. Suppose that Dr. P conducted an experiment showing that upside-down faces of dogs are recognized more easily by subjects if they bark three times while turning around in circles than if they don't. He claims to have replicated the experiment several times in his laboratory. Unfortunately, no one else has ever been able to replicate the effect. Give as many reasons as you can from the chapter to account for this.

√ EXERCISES AND APPLICATIONS

1. Consider the following statement from Chapter 1: "Research has discovered that we are not always privy to our own decision-making processes (Nisbett & Wilson, 1977)..." In one of several demonstrations illustrating nonscientific inference, Nisbett & Wilson had people rate their preferences for articles of clothing. The data showed that clothing on the person's right was strongly preferred over clothing on the left. When queried about this, "virtually all subjects denied it..." (p. 244).

    (a) Look up the reference for this article from the reference section of your textbook, and locate the article at the library. Explain briefly what Nisbett and Wilson actually did in this experiment, which begins on p. 243, and report the major findings.

    Position Effects experiment:

    (b) Another interesting experiment showing how people can be unaware of the real factors influencing their judgments appears on p. 244. Explain what Nisbett and Wilson did in this experiment and what they found.

    Personality experiment:

2. Over the next week, try to be aware of people's tendencies to make nonscientific inferences, such as those described in Nisbett & Wilson (1977). Describe two instances in which you observed yourself or someone else making a nonscientific inference.

Observation 1:

Observation 2:

√ RESEARCH IDEAS

1. People often act as though they believe in a myth, superstition, or fallacy. For example, do you ever find yourself avoiding walking under a ladder or stepping on a crack in the sidewalk even though you aren't superstitious?

    (a) It would be possible to conduct an experiment to find out whether people engage in superstitious behavior when it comes to walking under ladders. Create two sets of antecedent conditions (treatments) you could use to test whether people will walk out of their way to avoid going under a ladder. Describe the two treatment conditions you would use.

    <u>Treatment 1</u>   <u>Treatment 2</u>

    (b) Ask 10 of your friends to write down all of the superstitions they can think of in five minutes. Rank order the 5 superstitions that were mentioned most often. What problems did you encounter?

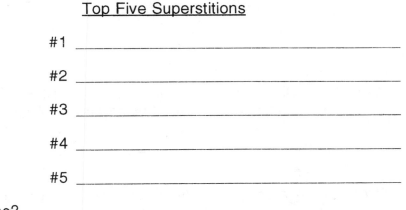

                    <u>Top Five Superstitions</u>

                    #1 _____

                    #2 _____

                    #3 _____

                    #4 _____

                    #5 _____

    (c) Problems?

23

2. Read your daily horoscope every morning on Monday through Friday. At the end of each day, rate how accurate you thought the day's horoscope was by circling one number on the scale.

<u>Monday</u>

| Very Inaccurate -2 | Somewhat Inaccurate -1 | Both Accurate and Inaccurate 0 | Somewhat Accurate +1 | Very Accurate +2 |

<u>Tuesday</u>

| Very Inaccurate -2 | Somewhat Inaccurate -1 | Both Accurate and Inaccurate 0 | Somewhat Accurate +1 | Very Accurate +2 |

<u>Wednesday</u>

| Very Inaccurate -2 | Somewhat Inaccurate -1 | Both Accurate and Inaccurate 0 | Somewhat Accurate +1 | Very Accurate +2 |

<u>Thursday</u>

| Very Inaccurate -2 | Somewhat Inaccurate -1 | Both Accurate and Inaccurate 0 | Somewhat Accurate +1 | Very Accurate +2 |

<u>Friday</u>

| Very Inaccurate -2 | Somewhat Inaccurate -1 | Both Accurate and Inaccurate 0 | Somewhat Accurate +1 | Very Accurate +2 |

When you have completed the scales, compute your average score.
(The second part of the project continues on the next page.)

3. During the next week, do not read your daily horoscope until the end of the day. Then rate how accurate you thought the day's horoscope was by circling one number on the scale.

Monday

| Very Inaccurate -2 | Somewhat Inaccurate -1 | Both Accurate and Inaccurate 0 | Somewhat Accurate +1 | Very Accurate +2 |

Tuesday

| Very Inaccurate -2 | Somewhat Inaccurate -1 | Both Accurate and Inaccurate 0 | Somewhat Accurate +1 | Very Accurate +2 |

Wednesday

| Very Inaccurate -2 | Somewhat Inaccurate -1 | Both Accurate and Inaccurate 0 | Somewhat Accurate +1 | Very Accurate +2 |

Thursday

| Very Inaccurate -2 | Somewhat Inaccurate -1 | Both Accurate and Inaccurate 0 | Somewhat Accurate +1 | Very Accurate +2 |

Friday

| Very Inaccurate -2 | Somewhat Inaccurate -1 | Both Accurate and Inaccurate 0 | Somewhat Accurate +1 | Very Accurate +2 |

When you have completed the research, compare your average scores from weeks 1 and 2. Use your findings to generate a testable hypothesis.

ANSWERS TO FILL-IN AND MULTIPLE CHOICE QUESTIONS

Fill-in

1. content (3)
2. process (3)
3. nonscientific (4)
4. trait (7)
5. stereotyping (8)
6. overconfidence (7)
7. faith in an organized universe (10)
8. empirical (10)
9. laws; theories (10, 11))
10. parsimony (11)
11. observed (15)
12. systematically (15)
13. measurement (17)
14. ethical (18)
15. antecedent conditions (19)
16. two (19)
17. equivalent (20)
18. temporal (20)
19. sufficient (21)

Multiple choice

1. c (3)
2. d (4)
3. b (7)
4. b (8)
5. b (8)
6. a (8)
7. a (9)
8. d (9)
9. a (11)
10. a (13)
11. b (14)
12. d (14)
13. a (15)
14. c (15)
15. c (19)
16. a (20)

SUGGESTED READINGS

Kahneman, D., Slovik, P., & Tversky, A. (1982). *Judgment under uncertainty: Heuristics and biases.* New York: Cambridge University Press.

Ross, L., & Nisbett, R. E. (1991). *The person and the situation: Perspectives of Social Psychology.* New York: McGraw-Hill.

Smith, R. A. (1995). *Challenging your preconceptions: Thinking critically about psychology.* Pacific Grove, CA: Brooks/Cole.

2 CHAPTER TWO
Research Ethics

Chapter Outline

√√ CHAPTER OBJECTIVES: KEY CONCEPTS

Listed below are questions that test the major concepts you should know from Chapter 2. After reading the chapter, you should be able to answer each of the questions below. If not, go back to the book and read the appropriate sections again before continuing on in the Study Guide.

_____

1. What are the factors that an institutional review board (IRB) takes into account when it conducts a risk/benefit analysis of a proposed experiment? (29)

2. What are the requirements for informed consent? (30)

3. What is meant by minimal risk research? (33)

4. What are the American Psychological Association guidelines governing the use of deception in research? (35)

5. Explain the difference between <u>anonymity and confidentiality</u>. (38)

 6. What is meant by the concept of <u>animal welfare</u>? (38)

7. How did <u>Coile and Miller's (1984) study</u> refute critics' extreme allegations of animal abuse? (42)

8. What is meant by the term <u>animal rights</u>, and how does it differ from <u>animal welfare</u>? (43)

9. What do we mean by <u>fraud</u> in published reports of psychological research, and what are three defenses against it? (46)

10. What is <u>plagiarism,</u> and how can you avoid it? (48)

√ QUESTIONS FOR REVIEW AND STUDY

KEY TERMS: define each term using your own words

Institutional review board (IRB) (29):

Risk/benefit analysis (29):

Informed consent (30):

Minimal risk (33):

Debriefing (36):

Animal welfare (38):

Institutional animal care and use committee (IACUC) (38):

Animal rights (43):

Fraud (46):

Plagiarism (48):

√ QUESTIONS FOR REVIEW AND STUDY

FILL INS: *fill in the blanks with the right word or phrase*

1. Research that is harmful to subjects is undesirable even though it may add to _____ .

2. The primary duty of an institutional review board is to ensure that _____ _____ is adequately protected.

3. _____ means any individual who may be exposed to the possibility of injury (physical, psychological, or social).

4. The determination that any risks to the individual are outweighed by potential benefits or the importance of the knowledge to be gained is called a _____ .

5. Informed consent means that the subject agrees to participate after having been fully informed about the _____ and _____ of the study.

6. Whenever there is any question concerning the ethics of an experiment, the researcher should seek advice from _____ or from _____ .

7. Research that does not alter the participants' odds of being harmed is considered _____ research.

8. Currently, some form of deception is used in approximately _____ % of psychological studies.

9. Whether the effects of deception can ever be fully reversed by _____ remains a serious ethical question.

10. Data should be collected _____ and kept _____ .

11. APA's CARE has been influential in establishing national guidelines for _____ .

12. Coile and Miller (1984) found that the actual percentage of articles that reported animal abuse, such as mutilation to produce behavioral change, was _____ %.

13. _____ is the idea that all sensate species, particularly those who can feel pain, are of equal value.

14. Before 1987, the E in CARE stood for _____; it now stands for _____ .

15. When we think of fraud in science, we typically think about researchers who _____ .

16. The consequences of _____ can range from suspension or firing by a university to a prison term if convicted in court.

17. If you have done a thorough review of the literature, your research report should contain many _____ .

Correct answers are located at the end of the chapter, but do not look at them until you have completed the test.

33

√ QUESTIONS FOR REVIEW AND STUDY

MULTIPLE CHOICE: *circle the best answer to each question*

1. The researcher's major concern in conducting research with human subjects is treating them _____ .
   a. morally and considerately
   b. harmlessly and painlessly
   c. kindly and gently
   d. ethically and responsibly

2. The <u>first</u> task of an IRB is to decide whether the proposed study _____.
   a. puts subjects at risk
   b. adds to the store of knowledge
   c. justifies the risks to subjects
   d. is well-designed

3. A procedure to determine whether the importance of an experiment outweighs potential harm to subjects is called _____ .
   a. an at risk analysis
   b. a risk/benefit analysis
   c. informed consent
   d. an APA guideline

4. John was asked to fill out an anonymous survey about his music preferences. This is an example of research that includes _____ .
   a. minimal risk to subjects
   b. subjects at risk
   c. an ethical dilemma
   d. deception and debriefing

5. Most researchers would agree that deception is justified if _____.
   a. subjects would not consent to participate if told the truth
   b. the principle of full disclosure is adhered to
   c. it is the only way to study a psychological problem
   d. subjects are debriefed at the end of the experiment

34

6. The debriefing experiment by Donnerstein and Berkowitz demonstrated that a(n) _____ was required to remove the negative consequences of viewing violent pornography.
    a. simple debriefing
    b. extensive debriefing
    c. 2- to 4-month follow-up
    d. full disclosure

7. Identifying subjects by code numbers instead of names is a way of protecting their _____ .
    a. safety
    b. welfare
    c. anonymity
    d. confidentiality

8. The care and treatment of animals in research is regulated by _____ .
    a. the Animal Welfare Act
    b. the A.S.P.C.A.
    c. People for the Ethical Treatment of Animals (PETA)
    d. the Humane Society

9. Which of the following was not a criticism of Brady's experiment?
    a. Electric shock was used to condition the monkeys.
    b. A poor research design decreased any potential benefits from the study.
    c. Some of the monkeys were so stressed they developed ulcers.
    d. The monkeys were deprived of food for extensive periods of time.

10. APA's ethical standards for animal care cover all of the following except _____ .
    a. humane treatment
    b. minimizing pain and suffering
    c. training and supervising research assistants
    d. prohibition against using electric shock

11. Coile and Miller (1984) found that _____ .
    a. in some psychology experiments, animals' limbs were amputated
    b. not a single extreme claim by animal activists was supported
    c. several studies were done merely to satisfy idle curiosity
    d. inescapable shocks were used in 60% of the studies

12. Which of the following best captures the concept of animal rights?
    a. Animal research is acceptable if it furthers our understanding of human behavioral principles.
    b. Animals may be used in psychological research only if the research promotes the welfare of human beings.
    c. All creatures capable of feeling pain are of equal value and have equal rights.
    d. Humans do not have the right to take the life of another animal.

13. According to Miller, animal research has led to treatments for all of the following psychological disorders except _____ .
    a. multiple personality disorder
    b. obsessive-compulsive disorder
    c. depression
    d. anorexia nervosa

14. Before 1987, the E in APA's CARE stood for _____ .
    a. exploitation
    b. experimentation
    c. ethics
    d. environment

15. Which of the following is not considered a form of fraud?
    a. fabricating data
    b. falsifying results
    c. accepting federal grants
    d. plagiarism

16. Which of the following is considered a form of plagiarism?
    a. paraphrasing someone else's ideas
    b. forgetting to give credit for ideas
    c. using direct quotes
    d. citing information that is common knowledge

17. A research report that contains many citations _____ .
    a. shows the reader that you are knowledgeable about your topic
    b. suggests that you need to look to others for ideas
    c. shows that you have not paraphrased statements made by others
    d. is less likely to be published than one with fewer citations

Correct answers are located at the end of the chapter, but do not look at them until you have completed the test.

√ QUESTIONS FOR REVIEW AND STUDY

SHORT ESSAY: use the information in the chapter to answer the following questions

1. Explain the functions of an institutional review board.

2. Why is knowledge about research methods important for conducting ethical experiments?

3. Explain the APA guidelines for "informed consent."

4. Explain when the use of deception might be appropriate in an experiment.

5. What do we mean by animal welfare? How is the concept of animal rights different?

6. What are the three lines of defense against fraud in psychological research?

√ EXERCISES AND APPLICATIONS

1. The complete revision of the American Psychological Association's "Ethical Principles of Psychologists and Code of Conduct" can be located in the December 1992 issue of *American Psychologist*, published by APA. Locate a copy from your library (or you might ask to borrow the journal from a professor who is an APA member), and photocopy it. Principles 6.06 through 6.26 apply to the ethics of conducting psychological research. Standards for psychologists who provide therapy, conduct training programs, teach psychology, and conduct forensic assessments can be found among the other principles listed.

    Consider the following proposed study: A clinical psychologist wants to bring her therapy patients into the laboratory for interviews about traumatic incidents in their past. The interviews will be conducted by graduate students, and each patient will be videotaped by hidden camera, so that the psychologist and her students can assess patients' degree of anxiety later by coding their body language. She has predicted that patients who show less anxiety will have better therapeutic outcomes.

    A number of ethical issues would need to be resolved before the psychologist could conduct this study. Using the ethical guidelines, find as many as you can. Then describe what additional safeguards would be needed. Cite each principle that applies.

2. Institutional review boards at colleges and universities frequently review proposals from researchers in many different departments--not only psychology. Obtain a copy of the form used to submit a proposed study to your IRB.

    (a) How do the guidelines listed for obtaining informed consent stack up with APA's guidelines? Do they include additional requirements not in APA's guidelines? If so, what are they?

    (b) Are they missing any of APA's principles for informed consent? If so, describe what is missing and which principles apply.

3. Talk to several people this week who believe in animal rights. Find out whether they (1) ever wear leather, (2) eat eggs, meat, poultry, or fish, or (3) own pets, and, if so, what they feed them. Compare the responses you collected with those of your classmates. What did you discover?

√ RESEARCH IDEAS

1. (a) With the permission of your instructor, use the questions below to construct a survey of people's knowledge about the use of animals in psychological research. Compare the answers from five people who advocate animal rights (as described in the chapter) with the answers of five people who do not and five who are not sure. Which group gave answers closer to the figures reported by Coile and Miller (1984) in your textbook?

    (b) Before you conduct the survey, decide how to handle the following ethical issues: Does the survey place subjects at risk? Should you get informed consent first? Will a debriefing be needed?

Animal Experimentation Survey

1. What percent of psychology experiments conducted on animals have used electric shock? _____ %

2. Some psychology experiments have deprived animals of food and water for certain periods of time. In these studies, what percent deprived the animals for more than 24 hours? _____ %

3. What percent of psychology experiments have inflicted pain or stress on animals just to satisfy a researcher's idle curiosity? _____ %

4. What percent of psychology experiments have allowed animals to become insane or even die in isolation chambers? _____ %

5. What percent of psychology experiments conducted on animals have either smashed their bones or intentionally ruptured their internal organs in order to study the effects on animal behavior? _____ %

6. Do you agree or disagree with the following statement?
    "It is acceptable to sacrifice the life of a baboon if transplanting its heart will extend the life of a human being."
    (Circle one)   I agree   I'm not sure   I disagree

Use item 6 to place the respondents into three animal rights groups (supporters, unsure, nonsupporters).

41

(c) Use the tally sheet to record each respondent's answers, and compute the average score for each group on items 1 through 5.

TALLY SHEET

	ITEM: #1	#2	#3	#4	#5
Supporter#1	____	____	____	____	____
Supporter#2	____	____	____	____	____
Supporter#3	____	____	____	____	____
Supporter#4	____	____	____	____	____
Supporter#5	____	____	____	____	____
Average	____	____	____	____	____
Unsure#1	____	____	____	____	____
Unsure#2	____	____	____	____	____
Unsure#3	____	____	____	____	____
Unsure#4	____	____	____	____	____
Unsure#5	____	____	____	____	____
Average	____	____	____	____	____
Nonsupporter#1	____	____	____	____	____
Nonsupporter#2	____	____	____	____	____
Nonsupporter#3	____	____	____	____	____
Nonsupporter#4	____	____	____	____	____
Nonsupporter#5	____	____	____	____	____
Average	____	____	____	____	____

(d) For each question, rank order the groups (*S, U,* and *NS*) from most to least accurate (*#1* = most accurate, *#2* is next, and *#3* is least accurate).

ITEM :	1	2	3	4	5
#1	____	____	____	____	____
#2	____	____	____	____	____
#3	____	____	____	____	____

(e) What is your conclusion about the relationship between attitudes and accuracy?

(f) What problems did you encounter?

ANSWERS TO FILL-IN AND MULTIPLE CHOICE QUESTIONS

Fill-in

1. the store of knowledge (28)
2. the safety of research participants (29)
3. subject at risk (29)
4. risk/benefit analysis (29)
5. nature; purpose (30)
6. an IRB; colleagues (32)
7. minimal risk (33)
8. 60% (33)
9. debriefing (36)
10. anonymously; confidential (38)
11. animal welfare (39)
12. 0.0% (43)
13. animal rights (43)
14. experimentation; ethics (45)
15. publish false data (46)
16. scientific misconduct (48)
17. citations (48)

Multiple choice

1.	d (28)	10.	d (40)
2.	a (29)	11.	b (42)
3.	b (29)	12.	c (43)
4.	a (33)	13.	a (43)
5.	c (35)	14.	b (45)
6.	b (37)	15.	c (46)
7.	c (37)	16.	b (48)
8.	a (38)	17.	a (48)
9.	d (39)		

SUGGESTED READINGS

American Psychological Association. (1982). *Ethical principles in the conduct of research with human participants.* Washington, DC: Author.

Jung, J. (1971). *The experimenter's dilemma.* New York: Harper & Row:

3 CHAPTER THREE
Alternatives to Experimentation: Nonexperimental Designs

Chapter Outline

√√ CHAPTER OBJECTIVES: KEY CONCEPTS

Listed below are questions that test the major concepts you should know from Chapter 3. After reading the chapter, you should be able to answer each of the questions below. If not, go back to the book and read the appropriate sections again before continuing on in the Study Guide.

---

1. When are <u>nonexperimental methods</u> used? What four approaches are covered in the chapter? (54)

2. Explain what the following phrases mean: <u>degree of manipulation of antecedents</u>; <u>degree of imposition of units</u>. (55)

3. What is <u>phenomenology</u>? (56)

4. Describe the problems inherent in the <u>case study approach</u>. (61)

5. What is a <u>field study</u>? Give an example. (63)

6.   Explain what is meant by the term <u>naturalistic observation</u>. (63)

7.   What are the unique problems posed by a <u>participant-observer study</u>? (67)

8.   Describe <u>open-ended and closed questions</u> used in survey research, and give an example of each. (69)

9.   What are the three <u>response styles</u>, and how can you control for them? (73)

10.   Describe three types of <u>probability sampling</u> procedures. (77)

11.   Describe two types of <u>nonprobability sampling</u> procedures. (80)

√ QUESTIONS FOR REVIEW AND STUDY

KEY TERMS: *define each term using your own words*

Internal validity (54):

External validity (54):

Phenomenology (56):

Case study (58):

Deviant case analysis (61):

Retrospective data (61):

Field study (63):

Naturalistic observation (63):

Systematic observation (65):

Reactivity (66):

Unobtrusive measures (66):

Participant-observer study (67):

Survey research (69):

Content analysis (71):

Response styles (73):

Willingness to answer (73):

Position preference (73):

Yea-sayers/Nay-sayers (74):

Sampling (75):

Population (75):

Sample of subjects (75):

Representativeness (75):

Probability sampling (77):

Random selection (77):

Simple random sampling (77):

Random number table (78):

Stratified random sampling (79):

Cluster sampling (80):

Nonprobability sampling (80):

Quota sampling (81):

Convenience sampling (81):

√ QUESTIONS FOR REVIEW AND STUDY

FILL INS: *fill in the blanks with the right word or phrase*

_____

1. Laboratory experiments can be high in _____ validity, but are often low in _____ validity.

2. When an experiment is not feasible or desirable, researchers can use _____ approaches.

3. Describing our own immediate experience is called _____.

4. Clinical psychologists, in particular, have relied heavily on the _____ approach.

5. A research method that compares histories from normal and abnormal individuals is called a _____.

6. Case studies frequently rely on _____ data--a serious problem.

7. In naturalistic observation studies, researchers can quantify their observations by using the technique called _____.

8. One way of controlling for reactivity is to use _____ measures.

9. A researcher who becomes part of the group being studied is conducting a _____ study.

51

10. The two most common survey techniques are _____ and _____.

11. Asking subjects why they like to watch TV would be an example of a(n) _____ question.

12. Willingness to answer is one form of _____ .

13. _____ refers to how closely a sample mirrors the population from which it was selected.

14. Field research using data from films, newspapers, and magazines is a form of _____ study.

15. To obtain a _____ sample, all members of the population must have an equal chance of being selected.

16. A researcher who draws prospective subjects' names out of a hat to decide who will participate in an experiment is using _____ selection.

17. Research conducted on a sample of people from a local nursing home is using a _____ (or accidental) sample.

18. When reporting samples, researchers include _____ information, such as gender, age, and education ranges, when they are important for interpreting the results.

Correct answers are located at the end of the chapter, but do not look at them until you have completed the test.

√ QUESTIONS FOR REVIEW AND STUDY

MULTIPLE CHOICE: circle the best answer to each question

1. A researcher who wanted to study the influence of gender on behavior would be using the _____ .
   a. experimental approach
   b. nonexperimental approach
   c. observed differences situation
   d. real-life situation

2. Where in our graphic scheme of research activities (Figure 3-1) would phenomenology fall?
   a. low-low
   b. low-high
   c. high-high
   d. high-low

3. Which of the following is not a purpose served by case studies?
   a. a source of hypotheses
   b. provide exceptions to accepted ideas
   c. a source of therapy techniques
   d. a substitute for laboratory research

4. To be diagnosed with antisocial personality disorder, an individual is likely to exhibit all of the following except _____ .
   a. a lack of true remorse
   b. a childhood history of problems with school and authorities
   c. an adult history of illegal, destructive, and irresponsible behaviors
   d. being born a twin or one of a set of triplets

5. Which of the following is true of naturalistic observation?
   a. It is explanatory rather than descriptive.
   b. It can include the manipulation of antecedents.
   c. Subjects' responses are free to vary.
   d. It has been used most often with mental patients.

6. INTERSECT is a form of _____ .
   a. systematic observation
   b. naturalistic observation
   c. participant-observer study
   d. field study

7. The tendency to alter behavior or responses when an individual is aware of being observed is known as _____ .
   a. willingness to answer
   b. yea-saying
   c. reactivity
   d. *feng shui*

8. Data gathered in participant-observer studies tend to be _____ .
   a. obtrusive
   b. systematic
   c. qualitative
   d. objective

9. Which of the following was not one of the results reported by Bechtol and Williams (1977)?
   a. Littering was greatest during the summer.
   b. Subjects all said they did not litter the beach.
   c. Subjects reported that they were disturbed about the amount of litter.
   d. Subjects said that they frequently saw others litter.

10. Closed questions are generally preferred to open-ended questions because the answers are easier to _____ .
    a. qualify
    b. quantify
    c. measure
    d. remember

11. A survey researcher would not want to use the question "Do you believe pet owners should have the right to end the tragic misery of their suffering pets by painlessly and humanely euthanizing them" because it is _____ .
    a. value laden
    b. too complex
    c. too ambiguous
    d. uninvolving

12. Which of the following was not given as one of the potential problems with giving questionnaires in group sessions?
    a. People may not take the survey as seriously.
    b. Subjects might not feel that they are anonymous.
    c. Sensitive questions might cause more embarrassment.
    d. Subjects might spend too much time talking with their friends.

13. When constructing questions or test items, researchers need to consider personal characteristics of subjects, called _____ , that can alter the way they answer questions regardless of the content.
   a. representativeness
   b. reactivity
   c. response sets
   d. response styles

14. When designing questions that require yes or no answers, researchers construct items that force people to think about their answers; this controls for _____ .
   a. position preference
   b. willingness to answer
   c. yea- and nay-saying
   d. manifest content

15. The results of interviews can be affected by all of the following except _____ .
   a. interviewer's appearance
   b. rapport
   c. interviewer consistency
   d. nonreturn rates

16. Selecting subjects so that the odds of their being in the study are known or can be calculated is called _____ .
   a. population sampling
   b. probability sampling
   c. stratified random sampling
   d. nonprobability sampling

17. Assume that a researcher wants to obtain a stratified random sample from people at a university, so that she can survey their attitudes about parking fees. She knows that there are 300 faculty, 185 staff people, 15 high-level administrators, and 14,500 students. She has 1,000 questionnaires to mail out randomly. How many questionnaires would go to randomly selected high-level administrators?
   a. 1
   b. 5
   c. 10
   d. 15

Correct answers are located at the end of the chapter, but do not look at them until you have completed the test.

√ QUESTIONS FOR REVIEW AND STUDY

_____

1. Discuss the tradeoffs between internal and external validity when using a nonexperimental approach to research.

2. Explain the two dimensions used in our graphic scheme in Figure 3-1 in the textbook.

3.	What have case studies been used for? What are the major problems
	with case studies?

4.	Explain the similarities and differences between (1) systematic
	observation and (2) content analysis.

5. What problems are inherent in field studies?

6. Explain how response styles can alter the ways subjects respond to the manifest content of questions.

√ EXERCISES AND APPLICATIONS

1. (a) Construct an eight-item questionnaire to measure <u>attitudes toward research in psychology</u>. Make up closed questions so that subjects can answer yes or no to each one. (The first and last items are provided, but you must make up the rest.) Be sure to control for each of the three kinds of response styles discussed in the chapter.

Attitudes Toward Psychological Research Questionnaire

1. I strongly support the idea that psychologists should conduct research to investigate psychological problems. (Circle one: yes   no   )

2.

3.

4.

5.

6.

7.

8. I have never known anyone very well who has had serious psychological problems. (Circle one: yes   no   )

   (b) To explore the issue further, add an open question of your own as item 9. (To quantify responses to this question, you would need to perform a content analysis of this item. How would you go about it?)

9.

(The exercise continues on the next page.)

(c) Many kinds of personal and demographic factors would be expected to influence people's answers to this questionnaire. Add 10 items to the end of your questionnaire that would provide you with additional information. The first item is provided.

1. Years of school completed: _____   6.

2.   7.

3.   8.

4.   9.

5.   10.

(d) Before you could ask people to fill out your questionnaire, what ethical issues would you need to consider? (How would you handle them?)

(e) What type of sampling procedure would provide the greatest amount of external validity for this survey?

(f) How much generalizability would the survey have if you gave the questionnaire to 20 of your friends and relatives?

√ RESEARCH IDEAS

1. **Part one**. (a) Find a location where you can sit and observe people's behavior unobtrusively (and ethically) for a while. You might choose a fast-food restaurant, a shopping mall, the student center, or even a bowling alley. Record the different behaviors people engage in.

Naturalistic Observation

Place_____ Date _____ Time _____

Behaviors:

(Use additional sheets of paper if needed.)

(b) Generate a testable hypothesis for one of the common behaviors you see. (One example of a hypothesis easily tested through observation is: Women order smaller ice cream cones when they are with an opposite-sex person than when they are with a same-sex person; but you need to make up a hypothesis of your own.)

Hypothesis: _____

_____

(c) Your hypothesis should include two variables that you can measure. (In the above example, women's weight (thin or obese) and the number of scoops (one, two, three, etc.) are the two variables. How will you categorize and quantify your variables so that they can be measured?

Variable 1 _____

Variable 2 _____

(The second part of the study continues on the next page.)

61

Part two. (a) Return to the same place at about the same time of day. Record the measurements of your variables for twenty subjects.

	Var. 1	Var. 2		Var. 1	Var. 2
S1	_____	_____	S11	_____	_____
S2	_____	_____	S12	_____	_____
S3	_____	_____	S13	_____	_____
S4	_____	_____	S14	_____	_____
S5	_____	_____	S15	_____	_____
S6	_____	_____	S16	_____	_____
S7	_____	_____	S17	_____	_____
S8	_____	_____	S18	_____	_____
S9	_____	_____	S19	_____	_____
S10	_____	_____	S20	_____	_____

(b) Did you assign numbers to represent different amounts or categories in both variables? (For example, in the earlier example, you could use the following scheme: 1 = thin; 2 = obese; scoops already have a number: 1, 2, etc.) If not, replace your record with the appropriate numbers you have assigned.

(c) Group your findings by variable, similar to our example, as follows:

		Type of Subject		*Your Variable 1*
		Thin	Obese	
	1	7	3	
# of Scoops	2	2	5	*Your Variable 2*
	3	1	2	

(d) Examine the groupings. Does it look as if your hypothesis was supported? Why? (Keep in mind that you cannot know for certain unless you actually conduct statistical analyses.)

(e) Was this a field study or a field experiment? Explain your answer.

ANSWERS TO FILL-IN AND MULTIPLE CHOICE QUESTIONS

Fill-in

1. internal; external (54)
2. nonexperimental (54)
3. phenomenology (56)
4. case study (58)
5. deviant case analysis (61)
6. retrospective (61)
7. systematic observation (65)
8. unobtrusive (66)
9. participant-observer (67)
10. questionnaires; interviews (69)
11. open-ended (69)
12. response style (73)
13. representativeness (75)
14. archival (76)
15. simple random (77)
16. random (77)
17. convenience (81)
18. demographic (82)

Multiple choice

1. b (54)
2. a (56)
3. d (58)
4. d (62)
5. c (63)
6. a (65)
7. c (66)
8. c (67)
9. d (68)
10. b (71)
11. a (71)
12. b (72)
13. d (73)
14. c (74)
15. d (74)
16. b (77)
17. a (78)

SUGGESTED READINGS

Breakwell, G. M., Hammond, S., & Fife-Shaw, C. (1995). *Research methods in psychology* (Chapters 8, 12, and 14). Thousand Oaks, CA: Sage.

Rosenhan, D. L. (1973). On being sane in insane places. *Science, 179,* 250-258.

Turnbull, C. M. (1961). Some observations regarding the experiences and behavior of the BaMbuti Pygmies. *American Journal of Psychology, 74,* 304-308.

4 CHAPTER FOUR

Alternatives to Experimentation: Correlational and Quasi-Experimental Designs

Chapter Outline

√√ CHAPTER OBJECTIVES: KEY CONCEPTS

Listed below are questions that test the major concepts you should know from Chapter 4. After reading the chapter, you should be able to answer each of the questions below. If not, go back to the book and read the appropriate sections again before continuing on in the Study Guide.

----

1.   Why are <u>correlational and quasi-experimental designs</u> lower in internal validity but usually higher in external validity than true experiments? (89)

2.   How does <u>correlation</u> improve upon simple observation? (90)

3.   What is a <u>correlation</u>? What is a <u>linear regression analysis</u>? (90, 94)

4.   Describe how the direction and strength of a relationship can be seen in a <u>scatterplot</u>. (91)

5.   When two variables are correlated, there are four possible <u>causal directions</u>. Describe all four. (94, 95)

6.   How is a <u>multiple correlation</u> different from a simple correlation? (96)

7. Describe the information produced by a factor analysis. (98)

8. How do path analysis and cross-lagged panels work? What are their limitations? (100)

9. When can a researcher use a quasi-experimental design? (102)

10. Explain the advantages and disadvantages of using the ex post facto design. (104)

11. Explain why the ex post facto study described in Box 4-3 failed to prove that big cars are safer than small cars (107)

12. What are the differences between a longitudinal and a cross-sectional study? (108, 110)

13. What are the limitations of the pretest/posttest design? (111)

KEY TERMS: *define each term using your own words*

Correlational study (90):

Correlation (90):

Scatterplot (91):

Regression line (91):

Positive correlation (92):

Negative correlation (92):

Coefficient of determination (94):

Linear regression analysis (94):

Multiple correlation (96):

Multiple regression analysis (97):

Causal modeling (97):

Path analysis (97):

Cross-lagged panel (100):

Quasi-experimental design (102):

Ex post facto study (104):

Subject variable (104):

Pretest/posttest design (108):

Longitudinal design (108):

Cross-sectional study (110):

√ QUESTIONS FOR REVIEW AND STUDY

FILL INS: **fill in the blanks with the right word or phrase**

1. Correlational designs are used to establish relationships among antecedents (traits, characteristics, events, or behaviors) that are _____.

2. _____ designs can be used when subjects cannot be randomly assigned to different treatment conditions.

3. As a group, correlational designs and quasi-experiments tend to be higher in _____ validity than true experiments.

4. The type of study used to determine the degree of relationship between two variables is called a _____ study.

5. The sign of a correlation coefficient tells the direction of the relationship; the absolute value tells the _____.

6. The correlation between admissions tests and college grades is an example of a _____ relationship.

7. When many items are measured, _____ can be used to form groups of related items.

8. In path analysis, different _____ can be compared to find the best causal model.

9. The most important correlations to consider in a cross-lagged panel are the two _____ .

10. The internal validity of quasi-experiments is lessened by the
_____ problem.

11. In a(n) _____ study, subjects are grouped on the
basis of preexisting differences.

12. A quasi-experiment in which the behaviors of the same subjects are
measured at different points in time is called a(n)
_____ design.

13. In the negative ion experiment described in Box 4-3, both moderate and
high levels of negative ions enhanced the aggressiveness of
_____ subjects, but had no effect on _____ subjects.

14. When choosing between a longitudinal and a cross-sectional study,
you need to keep in mind that cross-sectional studies require
_____ subjects.

15. The effects of practice, also called _____,
are an important consideration when using a pretest/posttest design.

16. A _____ design is often used to test the
effects of foreseeable real world events.

17. A design which includes three comparison groups in addition to a
pretest/posttest group is called a _____design.

**Correct answers are located at the end of the chapter, but do not
look at them until you have completed the test.**

√ QUESTIONS FOR REVIEW AND STUDY

MULTIPLE CHOICE: *circle the best answer to each question*

1. Which of the following is <u>not</u> one of the uses of correlational designs?
   a. to establish relationships among preexisting behaviors
   b. to predict one set of behaviors from another
   c. to propose causal models
   d. to manipulate antecedents

2. Both correlational and quasi-experimental designs tend to be _____ in the imposition of units.
   a. high-high
   b. low-high
   c. high
   d. low

3. In a correlational study, the degree of relationship is determined by _____.
   a. heuristic value
   b. statistical analysis
   c. practical and ethical reasons
   d. measuring many behaviors

4. When the dots in a scatterplot form a pattern that goes from upper left to lower right, it is a rough indication of a _____ relationship.
   a. weak
   b. positive
   c. direct
   d. negative

5. Which of the following correlation coefficients indicates the strongest relationship?
   a. -.67
   b. +2.4
   c. +.66
   d. 0.0

6. To evaluate the degree of relationship among three or more behaviors, researchers can use the technique called _____ .
   a. simple correlation
   b. regression analysis
   c. partial correlation
   d. multiple correlation

7. Path analysis can be used for all of the following except _____.
   a. testing effects over time
   b. predicting one event from another
   c. generating hypotheses
   d. proposing causal sequences

8. What is the name of the design in which subjects are measured at two different points of time on the same pair of variables?
   a. Path analysis
   b. Longitudinal study
   c. Cross-lagged panel
   d. Ex post facto

9. Quasi-treatment groups can be formed from all of the following except _____.
   a. traits and personality characteristics
   b. manipulated antecedents
   c. behaviors people engage in
   d. naturally-occurring life events

10. A major difference between experiments and quasi-experiments is that in quasi-experiments_____.
    a. the experimenter cannot randomly assign people to treatments
    b. the treatments take place outside of the laboratory
    c. subjects cannot be exposed to different treatments
    d. third variables are carefully controlled

11. The study by Franklin, Janoff-Bulman, and Roberts (1990) found that students of divorced parents had more pessimistic beliefs about their own potential success in marriage. This is an example of a(n) _____ study.
    a. correlational
    b. cross-lagged panel
    c. longitudinal
    d. ex post facto

12. Which of the following is the <u>best</u> way to describe the results of the car study reported in Box 4-2?
    a. Large cars are safer than small cars.
    b. Luxury cars and vans are safer than Corvettes.
    c. Cars with air bags resulted in fewer deaths than cars without air bags.
    d. Death rates were lower for drivers of large cars than for drivers of small cars.

13. In longitudinal studies, a researcher measures _____ .
    a. different subjects at the same time
    b. the same subjects at different times
    c. the same related variables at different times
    d. the same subjects before and after treatment

14. Compared with cross-sectional studies, longitudinal studies _____ .
    a. have greater internal validity
    b. take less time to complete
    c. require fewer subjects
    d. use less powerful statistical techniques

15. A researcher at a weight-management center who wanted to study the effects of subliminal self-help tapes on weight control would probably use a(n) _____ design.
    a. ex post facto
    b. cross-sectional
    c. pretest/posttest
    d. longitudinal

16. A major problem with pretest/posttest designs is the possibility of _____ effects.
    a. practice
    b. posttest desensitization
    c. preparation
    d. trait or personality

Correct answers are located at the end of the chapter, but do not look at them until you have completed the test.

√ QUESTIONS FOR REVIEW AND STUDY

SHORT ESSAY: use the information in the chapter to answer the following questions

1. Discuss the major differences between nonexperimental designs, such as correlations and quasi-experiments, and a true experiment. (Be sure to include *manipulation of antecedents* and *internal validity* in your answer.)

2. What does it mean to say that variable X and variable Y are strongly correlated? Why can't we say that X causes Y?

3.   Discuss the pros and cons of proposing causal models using a path
analysis. Use an example to help explain your answer.

4.   Explain how an ex post facto study is conducted, and discuss why you
cannot make a cause and effect statement using this design?

5.   Explain the *third variable problem* and how it relates to longitudinal and cross-sectional designs.

6.   Dr. H conducted a study to see if a controlled breathing procedure would reduce anxiety in the laboratory. He measured subjects' anxiety when they arrived at the laboratory and, again, after the breathing procedure. Subjects' average anxiety scores were much lower after the treatment. Can he be certain that his procedure caused the reduction in anxiety? Explain your answer.

√ EXERCISES AND APPLICATIONS

1. Imagine that a researcher found a strong correlation between temperature and the amount of violent crime in a large, urban city (r = +.55). He claimed that he had shown that hot weather causes people to commit more crimes. What is wrong with his statement?

2. For the study described above, list as many potential third variables as you can think of that might explain the results.

3.   Researchers* have found that fans of heavy metal music have lower *need for cognition* (nCog) scores than people who don't like heavy metal music. (The need for cognition represents how much we like to think and how much we like projects that require a lot of thinking.) Because of the design of the research, the study's authors were very careful not to make the statement that heavy metal music causes people to dislike thinking. Why couldn't they make that statement?

4.   For the study described above, list as many potential third variables as you can think of that might explain the differences between fans and nonfans.

*Hansen, C. H., & Hansen, R. D. (1991). Constructing personality and social reality through music: Individual differences among fans of punk and heavy metal music. *Journal of Broadcasting & Electronic Media, 35,* 335-350.

√ RESEARCH IDEAS

1. For the next week, keep a log of people's poor driving behaviors. Every time you notice a driver breaking the law or driving recklessly (speeding, making fast lane changes, running red lights, and so forth), write down the color of the car he or she was driving. To make the study manageable, code only lawbreakers in black or white cars, trucks, or vans. Tally your scores below.

    BLACK   WHITE

    (a) Did you observe more lawbreaking behaviors from cars of one particular color in this ex post facto study? Describe your results in a sentence that does not make a statement about cause and effect.

    (b) If differences were found, it does not necessarily mean that black cars (or white cars, if that was your study's top lawbreaking car color) caused people to drive more recklessly. List all the potential third variables you can. Only answers that are plausible will count. You cannot say, for instance, that all the radios in one color car might have been broken, making the drivers angry. That isn't likely. But, were the cars (or drivers, or both) actually different in some way that might have influenced your results? (E.g., if the black cars were mostly sports cars driven by people under 25, while the white cars were mostly sedans driven by people over 40, you would have some good potential third variables to list!)

2.   (a) Suppose a student measured 20 classmates on two different variables: the amount of time (in hours per week) they watched MTV, and the amount of time they spent studying for class. Use each pair of scores in the hypothetical data set for S_1 through S_{20}, provided below, to construct a scatterplot.

	MTV	Study		MTV	Study
S_1	4	8	S_{11}	1	7
S_2	6	6	S_{12}	20	3
S_3	2	10	S_{13}	2	6
S_4	3	9	S_{14}	4	3
S_5	12	4	S_{15}	2	12
S_6	5	5	S_{16}	3	8
S_7	7	6	S_{17}	2	11
S_8	3	8	S_{18}	7	4
S_9	1	10	S_{19}	3	8
S_{10}	3	10	S_{20}	4	5

Scatterplot:

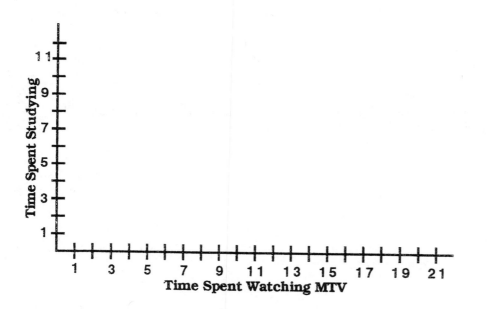

(The exercise continues on the next page.)

(b) Examine the scatterplot. Does it look like the correlation between time spent watching MTV and time spent studying is positive or negative?

(c) Does it look like the two variables are strongly or weakly related?

(d) The actual correlation between the two variables is $r = -.64$. You have learned in Chapter 4 that for any strong correlation between two variables there are four possible causal directions (p. 93). For this correlational study, what four cause and effect possibilities exist? The first is given below, but you need to state the remaining three.

1. Spending more time watching MTV causes less time to be spent studying.

2. _____

   _____

3. _____

   _____

4. _____

   _____

(e) Name two potential third variables that might be producing the association.

ANSWERS TO FILL-IN AND MULTIPLE CHOICE QUESTIONS

Fill-in

1. preexisting (87)
2. Quasi-experimental (87)
3. external (88)
4. correlational (89)
5. strength (90)
6. positive (92)
7. factor analysis (94)
8. regression equations (97)
9. diagonals (99)
10. third variable (100)
11. ex post facto (101)
12. longitudinal (106)
13. Type A; Type B (107)
14. more (108)
15. pretest sensitization (109)
16. pretest/posttest (109)
17. Solomon 4-group (110)

Multiple choice

1. d (90, 97)
2. c (90)
3. b (90)
4. d (92)
5. a (93)
6. d (96)
7. a (100)
8. c (100)
9. b (103)
10. a (103)
11. d (105)
12. d (107)
13. b (108)
14. c (110)
15. c (111)
16. a (111)

SUGGESTED READINGS

Hansen, C. H., & Hansen, R. D. (1991). Constructing personality and social reality through music: Individual differences among fans of punk and heavy metal music. *Journal of Broadcasting & Electronic Media, 35,* 335-350.

Zajonc, R. B., & Markus, G. B. (1975). Birth order and intellectual development. *Psychological Review, 82,* 74-88.

5 C H A P T E R F I V E
Formulating the Hypothesis

Chapter Outline

√√ CHAPTER OBJECTIVES: KEY CONCEPTS

Listed below are questions that test the major concepts you should know from Chapter 5. After reading the chapter, you should be able to answer each of the questions below. If not, go back to the book and read the appropriate sections again before continuing on in the Study Guide.

----

1.   How is a <u>nonexperimental hypothesis</u> different from an <u>experimental hypothesis</u>? (118)

2.   What is a <u>synthetic</u> statement, and why must a hypothesis be a synthetic (rather than analytic or contradictory) statement? (119)

3.   Explain what we mean by a <u>testable</u> hypothesis. (120)

4.   Why is it important that hypotheses be worded so that they are <u>falsifiable</u>? (121)

5.   What is meant by the term <u>parsimonious</u> hypothesis? (121)

6.   What is a <u>fruitful</u> hypothesis? (121)

7.   Explain how <u>induction</u> is used to generate hypotheses, and give an example. (123)

8.   What does the statement "Induction is the basic tool of <u>theory</u> building" mean? (123)

9.   Describe the <u>deductive model</u> of forming hypotheses. (124)

10. How can induction and deduction be <u>combined</u> in theory building? (125)

11. How can hypotheses come about through <u>serendipity</u>? (127)

12. Describe what is meant by <u>intuition</u>, and explain when it is most helpful for generating hypotheses. (129)

13. How would you begin a <u>literature search</u>? (133)

√ QUESTIONS FOR REVIEW AND STUDY

Hypothesis (118):

Nonexperimental hypothesis (118):

Experimental hypothesis (119):

Synthetic statement (119):

Analytic statement (120):

Contradictory statement (120):

Testable (120):

Falsifiable (121):

Parsimonious (121):

Fruitful (121)

Inductive model (123):

Deductive model (124):

Serendipity (127):

Intuition (129):

Psychological journal (132):

Meta-analysis (133)

Introduction (133):

Discussion (134):

√ QUESTIONS FOR REVIEW AND STUDY

FILL INS: fill in the blanks with the right word or phrase

1. Most psychological research is designed to test a _____.

2. A nonexperimental hypothesis predicts how events, traits, or behaviors might be _____.

3. An experimental hypothesis is a tentative _____ of an event or behavior.

4. If a statement can be either true or false, it is said to be a _____ statement.

5. An analytic statement is always _____; a contradictory statement is always _____ .

6. A statement of a research hypothesis must be disprovable, or _____ .

7. A hypothesis that leads to new studies is called _____ .

8. Reasoning from specific cases to more general principles uses the _____ model.

9. B. F. Skinner and Robert Zajonc proposed well-known theories based on _____ .

10. Reasoning from general principles to make predictions about specific instances uses the _____ model.

11. One way of finding hypotheses is to build on _____ research.

12. A good literature review will help you avoid _____ someone else's research.

13. Hypotheses that result from unplanned observations are said to come about through _____.

14. Nobel Prize winner Herbert Simon believes that intuition is most accurate when it comes from _____.

15. The hypotheses we form all of the time about the antecedent conditions that affect people's behavior are called _____.

16. One of the first steps in getting started on a research report is conducting a thorough _____.

17. A very useful statistical reviewing procedure that summarizes data from many similar studies is called a _____.

18. In the _____ section of your report, the results of an experiment are integrated into an existing body of knowledge.

19. Currently, psychologists' most important resource for finding journal articles is _____ , an electronic data base provided by the American Psychological Association.

Correct answers are located at the end of the chapter, but do not look at them until you have completed the test.

√ QUESTIONS FOR REVIEW AND STUDY

MULTIPLE CHOICE: *circle the best answer to each question*

1. Which of the following is <u>not</u> another word for the term hypothesis?
   a. thesis
   b. hunch
   c. guess
   d. statement

2. Which of the following research methods typically includes a hypothesis?
   a. phenomenology
   b. case study
   c. ex post facto
   d. survey

3. Every experimental hypothesis must be a(n) _____ statement.
   a. synthetic
   b. analytic
   c. contradictory
   d. antecedent

4. Which of the following statements is <u>not</u> testable?
   a. The length of time a dog sleeps is related to how much it eats.
   b. The happier the dog, the more it will wag its tail.
   c. The louder a dog barks, the more likely it is to bite.
   d. The bigger the dog, the dumber it is.

5. Chapter 6 describes different ways of testing the familiar adage "misery loves company" in an experiment. Therefore, it is <u>not</u> a(n) _____ statement.
   a. analytic
   b. parsimonious
   c. fruitful
   d. synthetic

6. The hypothesis that you will write an excellent research report if you follow all the guidelines in your textbook carefully enough is not _____ .
   a. parsimonious
   b. falsifiable
   c. provable
   d. formulated

7. Which of the following hypotheses is least parsimonious?
   a. Objects in a vacuum will fall at the same rate.
   b. People will tend to help more when alone than in groups.
   c. When treated inequitably by a female teacher in summer school, people will try to minimize their costs and maximize their rewards.
   d. High concentrations of negative ions increase the strength of both positive and negative moods.

8. The author has the hypothesis that her newest dog, Samson, is so dumb that he forgets who she is between the time she leaves for work and the time she gets home. One problem with this hypothesis is that it is probably not _____ .
   a. false
   b. provable
   c. fruitful
   d. analytic

9. From observing many instances of behavior, you generate a hypothesis about other behaviors you would expect from middle-aged men who drive red sports cars. In this instance, you would be using _____ .
   a. induction
   b. deduction
   c. common sense
   d. intuition

10. From reading about Zajonc's mere exposure theory, an advertiser predicted that people would come to like his client's new product if the client spent millions of dollars on a huge television advertising campaign. This advertiser is using _____ .
    a. causal attribution
    b. induction
    c. deduction
    d. both induction and deduction

11. Equity theory, proposed by Walster and her colleagues, actually came about through _____ .
    a. serendipity
    b. deduction
    c. induction
    d. both deduction and induction

12. The hypothesis that people will litter the beach less if they are provided with trash baskets resulted from _____ .
    a. serendipity
    b. intuition
    c. prior research
    d. both induction and deduction

13. Which of the following statements is not one of the recommended ways in which new hypotheses are generated from prior research?
    a. Additional variables that might mediate effects can be suggested.
    b. Replicating someone else's study can generate a new hypothesis.
    c. It can suggest new applications for previously tested hypotheses.
    d. Reading past research can focus your thinking on important issues.

14. Which of the following best characterizes what we mean by finding a research hypothesis through serendipity?
    a. Possessing the ability to be open to new possibilities.
    b. Knowing how to be happy about accidental findings.
    c. Abandoning old areas of research in favor of new opportunities.
    d. Having the wisdom to use an unplanned, but important, observation.

15. According to the text, when are our intuitive hypotheses most likely to be accurate?
    a. When we have strong psychic abilities.
    b. When we are experts in the area.
    c. When the hypothesis relates to our own behavior.
    d. When we are highly confident about our hunch.

16. Which of the following sources is not recommended when you search the literature for information about your topic?
    a. journal articles
    b. popular books and magazines
    c. research reviews
    d. a meta-analysis

Correct answers are located at the end of the chapter, but do not look at them until you have completed the test.

94

√ QUESTIONS FOR REVIEW AND STUDY

SHORT ESSAY: use the information in the chapter to answer the following questions

1. Describe the major differences between nonexperimental and experimental hypotheses.

2. Discuss the five characteristics of an experimental hypothesis.

3.   Explain the inductive and deductive models, and give an example of each.

4.   Use an example to describe how induction and deduction may be combined in research and theory-building.

5.   Describe several ways in which prior research can be useful in generating hypotheses.

6.   Explain how the information from a literature search is used in a research report.

1. Translate the following statements into the "If...then" form. Decide whether each one is an experimental (E) or nonexperimental (NE) hypothesis.

Misery loves company. _____
_____   E   NE

Child abusers tend to be people who were, themselves, abused as children. _____
_____   E   NE

Melatonin might be a cure for insomnia. _____
_____   E   NE

The frequency of SAD (seasonal affective disorder) across the U.S. is negatively correlated with the number of sunny days each year. _____
_____
_____   E   NE

Studying hard for 10 hours a week will get you an "A" in this course.
_____
_____   E   NE

Convicts who serve time in pink prison cells are paroled earlier than convicts who serve time in blue cells. _____
_____   E   NE

(The exercise continues on the next page.)

2.   (Only the first, third, fifth, and sixth statements could be tested in true experiments.) Ethical concerns aside, it would not be possible to manipulate the antecedent conditions for the second (creating subjects who were abused as children) and fourth (inducing SAD in subjects) hypotheses. Evaluate the four experimental hypotheses on the five characteristics of a good hypothesis. If the hypothesis meets the criterion, put a plus (+); if not, put a minus (-) in the appropriate column.

<u>Synthetic?</u>   <u>Testable?</u>   <u>Falsifiable?</u>   <u>Parsimonious?</u>   <u>Fruitful?</u>

Misery

Melatonin

Studying

Convicts

3.   Describe a research method you could use to investigate the nonexperimental hypotheses you generated for statements 2 and 4. Also, briefly explain how you would go about conducting an ethical study. What variables would you measure and how could you conduct the study so that the rights of the participants were protected?

Child abusers:

SAD:

√ RESEARCH IDEAS

1. From the data you collected from your naturalistic observation in Chapter 3, generate a testable, experimental hypothesis in the "If...then" form:

    _____

    _____

    _____

    _____

2. Use psycINFO to locate the reference for a journal article that appears to test your hypothesis (or one that is similar). Tape a copy of the reference information and abstract below.

3. Use psycINFO to retrieve two references for experiments testing the use of "light therapy" to help people with seasonal affective disorder. Write out the references in the proper format (discussed in detail in Chapter 16), which is given below with an example for you to follow.

APA style for listing journal articles as references:

Author(s) surname(s), and initial(s). The year of publication (in parentheses). Title of the article with only the first word capitalized. *The Name of the Journal, Volume number,* page numbers.

Hansen, C. H., & Hansen, R. D. (1991). Constructing personality and social reality through music: Individual differences among fans of punk and heavy metal music. *Journal of Broadcasting & Electronic Media, 35,* 335-350.

(a)_____

_____

_____

_____

_____

(b)_____

_____

_____

_____

_____

4. You should be able to get a sense of the hypothesis that was tested in an experiment from reading the psycINFO abstract. State the hypotheses tested in the articles you listed above.

(a)_____

_____

(b)_____

_____

Fill-in

1. hypothesis (118)
2. related (118)
3. explanation (119)
4. synthetic (119)
5. true; false (120)
6. falsifiable (121)
7. fruitful (121)
8. inductive (123)
9. induction (123, 124)
10. deductive (124)

11. prior (126)
12. duplicating (127)
13. serendipity (127)
14. experts (129)
15. causal attributions (132)
16. literature review (132)
17. meta-analysis (133)
18. discussion (134)
19. PsycINFO (134)

Multiple choice

1. d (118)
2. c (118)
3. a (119)
4. b (120)
5. a (120)
6. b (121)
7. c (121)
8. c (121)

9. a (123)
10. c (124)
11. d (125)
12. c (126)
13. b (126)
14. d (127)
15. b (129)
16. b (132)

SUGGESTED READINGS

Simon, H. A. (1967). Motivational and emotional controls of cognition. *Psychological Review, 74,* 29-39.

Weary, G., Stanley, M. A., & Harvey, J. H. (1989). *Attribution.* New York: Springer-Verlag.

2 P A R T   T W O

METHOD

The second major section of the textbook, called *Method,* parallels the Method section of a research report. The next six chapters will present a number of experimental research designs used by psychologists to investigate human and animal behavior and to test experimental hypotheses. You will learn that there are many kinds of experiments that can be conducted, depending on the research question that needs to be answered. Some designs test a hypothesis by comparing differences between groups of subjects exposed to different "treatments." Others test a hypothesis by comparing the behavior of a single group of subjects exposed to two or more different "treatments" in the same experiment. Some experimental designs require many subjects; others can be conducted with as few as one or two subjects. When experiments are conducted properly, researchers can make cause and effect statements about behavior--the goal of experimentation--using any one of the experimental designs you will be learning about.

By the time you have finished Part 2, you should be familiar with the most commonly used experimental designs. You should know (a) how to control for extraneous variables, (b) how to conduct experimental sessions, (c) how to conduct several different kinds of experiments, (d) when to use each of the different designs, and (e) the strengths and weaknesses of each technique. In Chapters 6 through 11, you will learn how the experimental method is applied to test hypotheses about the causes of behavior.

Chapter 6:   The Basics of Experimentation
Chapter 7:   Solving Problems: Controlling Extraneous Variables
Chapter 8:   Basic Between-Subjects Designs
Chapter 9:   Between-Subjects Factorial Designs
Chapter 10: Within-Subjects Designs
Chapter 11: Within-Subjects Designs: Small *N*

6 CHAPTER SIX
The Basics of Experimentation

Chapter Outline

✓✓ CHAPTER OBJECTIVES: KEY CONCEPTS

Listed below are questions that test the major concepts you should know from Chapter 6. After reading the chapter, you should be able to answer each of the questions below. If not, go back to the book and read the appropriate sections again before continuing on in the Study Guide.

_____

1.   What are the <u>independent</u> and <u>dependent variables</u> in an experiment? (144, 145)

2.   Describe the independent and dependent variables in <u>Schachter</u>'s experiment. In <u>Hess</u>'s. (147, 148)

3.   Explain what we mean by the term <u>experimental operational definition</u>. (152)

4.   Explain what we mean by the term <u>measured operational definition</u>. (153)

5.   What are <u>hypothetical constructs</u>, and how are they defined? (153)

6.　　Explain each of the <u>four levels of measurement</u> (nominal, ordinal, interval, and ratio), and describe how we select a level of measurement. (156)

7.　　Describe the three types of <u>reliability</u> (interrater, test-retest, and interitem reliability). (162)

8.　　Describe the five types of <u>validity</u> (face, content, predictive, concurrent, and construct validity). (163)

9.　　What is <u>internal validity</u>? (168)

10.　　What is the difference between an <u>extraneous variable</u> and a <u>confound</u>? Which one can invalidate an experiment? (168)

11.　　Describe the <u>eight classic threats</u> to internal validity. (173)

12.　　What information goes in the <u>Method</u> section of the report? (178)

√ QUESTIONS FOR REVIEW AND STUDY

KEY TERMS: *define each term using your own words*

Independent variable (IV) (144):

Environmental variable (144):

Task variable (144):

Levels of the independent variable (144):

Subject variable (145):

Dependent variable (145):

Operational definition (151):

Experimental operational definition (152):

Measured operational definition (153):

Hypothetical construct (153):

Scale of measurement (155):

Level of measurement (156):

Nominal scale (156):

Ordinal scale (156):

Interval scale (157):

Ratio scale (157):

Continuous dimension (160):

Reliability (161):

Interrater reliability (162):

Test-retest reliability (162):

Interitem reliability (162):

Validity (163):

Face validity (163):

Content validity (164):

Predictive validity (165):

Concurrent validity (165):

Construct validity (166):

Internal validity (168):

Extraneous variable (168):

Latent content (169):

Response set (169)

Confounding (171):

History threat (174):

Maturation threat (174):

Testing threat (175):

Instrumentation threat (175):

Statistical regression threat (176):

Selection threat (176):

Subject mortality threat (177):

Selection interaction threat (177):

Method section (178):

√ QUESTIONS FOR REVIEW AND STUDY

FILL INS: fill in the blanks with the right word or phrase

1. The dimension that the experimenter intentionally manipulates is called the _____ variable.

2. Each treatment condition represents one _____ of the IV.

3. We measure the effects of the independent variable on the _____ variable.

4. Each IV and each DV has two definitions--the conceptual definition and the _____ definition.

5. Schachter gave _____ operational definitions of high and low anxiety.

6. Schachter's dependent variable, affiliation, was given a _____ operational definition.

7. Unseen processes postulated to explain behavior are called hypothetical _____ .

8. A _____ scale has equal intervals between values and a true zero point.

9. The _____ scale was devised by Osgood, Suci, and Tannenbaum.

10. When different levels of measurement will fit equally well, choose the _____ level possible.

11. An operational definition that works the same way each time we apply it is said to be _____.

12. A dependent measure which fairly samples the quality we intend to measure is said to have _____ validity.

13. Variables in an experiment that are neither independent nor dependent variables are called _____ variables.

14. Variables that change in a systematic way across different conditions of an experiment are called _____.

15. Whenever you design or evaluate experimental research, you need to consider the eight classic threats to _____.

16. _____ is a threat to internal validity that is of particular concern in longitudinal studies that take months or years to finish.

17. A rubber ruler that stretches a bit every time you use it is an example illustrating an _____ threat to internal validity.

18. If your experiment required the use of specialized computer equipment, you would describe it in the _____ subsection of your report.

Correct answers are located at the end of the chapter, but do not look at them until you have completed the test.

QUESTIONS FOR REVIEW AND STUDY

MULTIPLE CHOICE: *circle the best answer to each question*

1. Which of the following is <u>not</u> a type of independent variable?
   a. environmental variable
   b. task variable
   c. subject variable
   d. extraneous variable

2. In an experiment to test whether people get higher grades on exams printed on blue paper or pink paper, what is the dependent variable?
   a. blue paper
   b. pink paper
   c. exam grades
   d. color of paper

3. The familiar adage "misery loves company" was tested by _____ .
   a. Dr. Gregor Zilstein
   b. Stanley Schachter
   c. Sarnoff and Zimbardo
   d. Niedenthal and Cantor

4. Operational definitions _____ .
   a. may change from one experiment to the next
   b. may have different meanings in the same experiment
   c. may have different meanings to different people
   d. are unchanging and standardized

5. We infer the existence of hypothetical constructs from _____ .
   a. observable behaviors
   b. internal sensations
   c. operational definitions
   d. baseline physiology

6. When Sarnoff and Zimbardo measured anxiety on a scale from 0 - 100, they were using a(n) _____ scale.
   a. nominal
   b. ordinal
   c. interval
   d. ratio

7. The _____ scale uses a set of bipolar adjectives.
   a. Likert
   b. Semantic Differential
   c. Likert-type
   d. Agreement-Disagreement

8. If your dependent variable can be measured equally well using any of the four levels of measurement, which one would be preferable to use?
   a. nominal
   b. ordinal
   c. interval
   d. ratio

9. Agreement between different observers taking measurements of the same behavior is called _____ .
   a. interrater reliability
   b. test-retest reliability
   c. interitem reliability
   d. internal consistency

10. A measure that produces about the same score each time a person is measured is said to have _____ .
    a. interrater reliability
    b. test-retest reliability
    c. interitem reliability
    d. internal consistency

11. When the validity of an operational definition is self-evident, the definition is said to have _____ validity.
    a. face
    b. content
    c. predictive
    d. construct

12. Winston Churchill was especially concerned with _____ validity.
    a. face
    b. content
    c. predictive
    d. construct

13. Extraneous variables can include all of the following except _____ .
    a. differences among subjects
    b. equipment failures
    c. task variables

d. inconsistent instructions

14. When subjects respond to the latent content of our questions, their goal may be a response set called _____ .
    a. self-description
    b. internal consistency
    c. face-saving
    d. social desirability

15. When an experiment is confounded, _____ .
    a. a gremlin is introducing nonsystematic variability into subjects' responses
    b. the dependent variable has probably produced an effect on the independent variable
    c. a causal relationship between the independent and dependent variables cannot be inferred
    d. the effects of the independent variable are obscured, making it harder to detect effects that may be present

16. A classic threat that refers to any internal changes in subjects that might have affected scores on the dependent measure is known as _____ .
    a. history
    b. maturation
    c. statistical regression
    d. subject mortality

17. If observers scored one condition of the experiment differently than another, internal validity is threatened by _____ .
    a. testing
    b. selection
    c. instrumentation
    d. regression toward the mean

18. The first subsection in Method is typically called _____ .
    a. Participants
    b. Apparatus
    c. Materials
    d. Measures

Correct answers are located at the end of the chapter, but do not look at them until you have completed the test

√ QUESTIONS FOR REVIEW AND STUDY

1. Describe the differences between independent and dependent variables.

2. Compare the operational definitions of anxiety used in Schachter's experiment with those used by Sarnoff and Zimbardo.

3. Explain the difference between a construct variable and a nonconstruct variable, and discuss how each kind of variable should be operationally defined.

4. Describe each of the four levels of measurement and give an example of each.

5.   What is reliability as it refers to an operational definition? Describe each of the three types presented in the text.

6.   What do we mean by the validity of an operational definition? Describe each of the five types presented in the text.

√ EXERCISES AND APPLICATIONS

1. In Chapter 3, you constructed items for a questionnaire called the *Attitudes Toward Psychological Research Questionnaire.*

    Your questions were scaled using a nominal scale of measurement (subjects could respond either yes or no). Now that you know more about the options for scaling questions, you know that researchers prefer to use higher scales of measurement (interval or ratio) when possible. Rework items 1 through 7 from your questionnaire so that the items use a Likert scale (see Box 6-1 in the text). Item 1 is provided.

    Attitudes Toward Psychological Research Questionnaire (Revised)

1. Psychologists should conduct research to investigate psychological problems.

    _____ strongly disagree
    _____ disagree
    _____ neutral
    _____ agree
    _____ strongly agree

2. _____

    _____

    _____ strongly disagree
    _____ disagree
    _____ neutral
    _____ agree
    _____ strongly agree

3. _____

    _____

    _____ strongly disagree
    _____ disagree
    _____ neutral
    _____ agree
    _____ strongly agree

4. _____

   _____

   _____   strongly disagree
   _____   disagree
   _____   neutral
   _____   agree
   _____   strongly agree

5. _____

   _____

   _____   strongly disagree
   _____   disagree
   _____   neutral
   _____   agree
   _____   strongly agree

6. _____

   _____

   _____   strongly disagree
   _____   disagree
   _____   neutral
   _____   agree
   _____   strongly agree

7. _____

   _____

   _____   strongly disagree
   _____   disagree
   _____   neutral
   _____   agree
   _____   strongly agree

8. I have never known anyone very well who has had serious psychological problems. (Circle one: yes   no)

Do not change item 8. Answers to item 8 could be used to group subjects into two levels of a subject variable: those who have known and those who have not known someone with serious psychological problems. You could now test whether these two groups of people differ in their answers to questionnaire items 1 through 7.

Answer the following questions about this possible study:

(a) Why would this be an ex post facto study--not a true experiment?

(b) An ex post facto study is similar to an experiment with a Selection threat to internal validity. Therefore, even if you found that responses differed a great deal between the two types of subjects, you could not say that knowing or not knowing someone with psychological problems caused them to answer differently. Using the idea of a Selection threat, explain why a causal inference cannot be made in this (or, for that matter, in any) ex post facto study.

2.   In Chapter 4, you learned about quasi-experimental designs, such as a longitudinal study, a cross-sectional study, and a pretest/posttest design. Which classic threat would most obviously threaten the internal validity of each of these research methods? (Illustrate each one with a brief example of what you mean.)

Longitudinal study:

Cross-sectional study:

Pretest/posttest design:

√ RESEARCH IDEAS

1. Look again at the experimental hypothesis that you generated in the **Research Ideas** section from the last chapter. Identify the independent and dependent variables and create an operational definition for each.

    (a) Independent variable:

    (b) Dependent variable:

2. For the last chapter, you also retrieved information from psycINFO about an article that tested a similar hypothesis. What were the independent and dependent variables in that experiment? (Typically, there is not enough space in the abstract to describe the experimental and measured operational definitions; these would be found in the published journal article.)

    (a) Independent variable:

    (b) Dependent variable:

ANSWERS TO FILL-IN AND MULTIPLE CHOICE QUESTIONS

Fill-in

1. independent variable (144)
2. level (144)
3. dependent (145)
4. operational (151)
5. experimental (152)
6. measured (153)
7. constructs (153)
8. ratio (157)
9. semantic differential (158)
10. highest (161)
11. reliable (161)
12. content (164)
13. extraneous (168)
14. confounds (171)
15. internal validity (173)
16. maturation (175)
17. instrumentation (175)
18. Apparatus (179)

Multiple choice

1. d (144)
2. c (145)
3. b (147)
4. a (151)
5. a (153)
6. c (157)
7. b (158)
8. d (161)
9. a (162)
10. b (162)
11. a (163)
12. b (164)
13. c (168)
14. d (169)
15. c (171)
16. b (174)
17. c (175)
18. a (178)

SUGGESTED READINGS

Cook, T. D., & Campbell, D. T. (1979). *Quasi-experimentation: Design and analysis issues for field settings.* Boston: Houghton Mifflin.

Sarnoff, I., & Zimbardo, P. G. (1961). Anxiety, fear, and social affiliation. *Journal of Abnormal and Social Psychology, 62,* 356-363.

Schachter, S. (1959). *The psychology of affiliation.* Stanford, CA: Stanford University Press.

7 CHAPTER SEVEN
Solving Problems: Controlling Extraneous Variables

Chapter Outline

√√ CHAPTER OBJECTIVES: KEY CONCEPTS

Listed below are questions that test the major concepts you should know from Chapter 7. After reading the chapter, you should be able to answer each of the questions below. If not, go back to the book and read the appropriate sections again before continuing on in the Study Guide.

_____

1.   Why is it important to control <u>extraneous variables</u>? (187)

2.   Explain what is meant by the term <u>physical variables</u>, and describe three techniques for handling them. (187)

3.   Describe <u>demand characteristics</u>, and explain how a <u>single-blind experiment</u> can help to control them. (191)

4.   What is the <u>placebo effect</u>? (196)

5.   Describe the advantages and disadvantages of a <u>cover story</u>. (197)

6.   Describe <u>experimenter bias</u> and give an example. (198)

7.   What is a <u>double-blind experiment</u>, and how does it control <u>experimenter bias</u>? (199)

8.   Explain the <u>Rosenthal effect</u>. (200)

9.   Describe some effects produced by <u>experimenters' personality variables</u>. (204)

10.   How can <u>personality variables associated with volunteers</u> influence validity? (205)

11.   What problems occur when <u>subjects select their own experiments</u>, and how can they be controlled? (206)

12.   What problems occur when <u>experimenters select their own subjects</u>, and how can they be controlled? (207)

13.   Explain the <u>folklore about subjects</u> (and the potential for similar problems with experimenters). (207)

KEY TERMS: *define each term using your own words*

Physical variables (187):

Elimination (188):

Constancy of conditions (188):

Balancing (189):

Social variables (191):

Demand characteristics (191):

Single-blind experiment (195):

Placebo effect (196):

Cover story (197):

Experimenter bias (198):

Rosenthal effect (199):

Double-blind experiment (202):

Personality variables (204):

Context variables (206):

FILL INS: fill in the blanks with the right word or phrase

---

1. Extraneous variables in an experiment, such as the day of the week or the amount of noise, are called _____ variables.

2. If we cannot eliminate an extraneous variable, we can use the second control procedure, called _____.

3. The technique of distributing effects of an extraneous variable across all the treatment conditions is called _____.

4. Qualities of the relationships between subjects and experimenters are known as _____ variables.

5. People often behave in ways they believe are expected of them; this problem is called _____.

6. Typically, subjects in experiments are extremely cooperative; this is known as the _____ phenomenon.

7. When subjects are not informed of their treatment condition, the experimenter is conducting a(n) _____ experiment.

8. Changes in behavior that can occur even when subjects are given the zero level of the independent variable are called a(n) _____ effect.

9. To control for guessing the real hypothesis, subjects are sometimes given a _____.

10. _____ occurs when experimenters give cues to subjects about how they should respond.

11. When experimenters "misread" scores or make recording errors, it is a form of _____.

12. Sometimes, subjects' behavior can be altered by expectations of the experimenter; this is called the _____ effect.

13. An excellent technique to control for experimenter effects is to conduct a(n) _____ study.

14. A likeable experimenter can produce better responses from subjects; this is an example of the influence of a(n) _____ variable.

15. Volunteer subjects tend to be less _____ than nonvolunteers.

16. Extraneous variables that relate to subject recruitment and selection are known as _____ variables.

17. Experimenters should devise a procedure ahead of time for _____ subjects and for _____ them to treatment conditions at random.

Correct answers are located at the end of the chapter, but do not look at them until you have completed the test.

√ QUESTIONS FOR REVIEW AND STUDY

MULTIPLE CHOICE: circle the best answer to each question

1. Physical variables include all of the following except _____ .
    a. the temperature of the laboratory room
    b. time of day
    c. the attractiveness of the subjects
    d. paintings on the walls of the testing room

2. Which of the following is <u>not</u> one of the ways to control extraneous physical variables?
    a. elimination
    b. systematizing
    c. constancy of conditions
    d. balancing

3. Allowing each subject the same amount of time to complete an experimental task is an example of _____ .
    a. elimination
    b. systematizing
    c. constancy of conditions
    d. balancing

4. If all the control subjects were tested in a bright, sunny room, and all the experimental subjects were tested in a dark, gloomy room, effects from the independent variable would be _____ .
    a. confounded
    b. unbalanced
    c. uncontrolled
    d. inconstant

5. Qualities of the relationships between subjects and experimenters are called _____ .
    a. extraneous variables
    b. physical variables
    c. social variables
    d. context variables

6.	When subjects respond according to how they think the experimenter wants them to, the experiment is contaminated by _____ .
	a.	context variables
	b.	demand characteristics
	c.	experimenter bias
	d.	the Rosenthal effect

7.	Martin Orne attributes the compliant attitude of research subjects to
	_____.
	a.	expectation bias
	b.	the Rosenthal effect
	c.	the Pollyanna effect
	d.	the "good subject" phenomenon

8.	Which of the following was manipulated by Orne and Scheibe in their "sensory deprivation" experiments?
	a.	demand characteristics
	b.	social variables
	c.	context variables
	d.	physical variables

9.	In a _____ experiment, subjects are not told by the experimenter what treatment condition they are in.
	a.	single-blind
	b.	double-blind
	c.	placebo group
	d.	control group

10.	Because subjects typically expect to get some kind of treatment, experimenters need to be aware of the possibility of _____ effects.
	a.	experimenter bias
	b.	placebo
	c.	Rosenthal
	d.	"good subject"

11.	One technique often used to keep subjects from guessing the hypothesis of the experiment is to use a _____.
	a.	single-blind study
	b.	double-blind study
	c.	placebo group
	d.	cover story

THE COLLEGE OF SAINT ROSE
432 WESTERN AVENUE
ALBANY, NEW YORK 12203-1490

Vice President for
Academic Affairs

12. All of the following are advantages of using a cover story except
_____ .
a. They control for demand characteristics.
b. They give subjects a hypothesis unrelated to the true hypothesis.
c. They keep subjects from guessing what will happen to them.
d. They create the same expectancy in all conditions of the experiment.

13. The Rosenthal effect is a particular kind of _____ .
a. experimenter bias
b. demand characteristic
c. "good subject" effect
d. placebo effect

14. For some reason, when experimenters make errors scoring or recording data, the errors tend to _____ .
a. favor certain kinds of subjects
b. favor the experimental hypothesis
c. occur more in control conditions
d. occur more in double-blind studies

15. A double-blind study can control all of the following except _____ .
a. the "good subject" phenomenon
b. an instrumentation threat
c. demand characteristics
d. experimenter bias

16. The likeability of an experimenter is one example of a _____ .
a. demand characteristic
b. Pygmalion effect
c. social variable
d. personality variable

17. Volunteers tend to have somewhat different personality characteristics than nonvolunteers. This can create problems with _____ .
a. experimenter bias
b. demand characteristics
c. internal validity
d. external validity

Correct answers are located at the end of the chapter, but do not look at them until you have completed the test.

√ QUESTIONS FOR REVIEW AND STUDY

SHORT ESSAY: use the information in the chapter to answer the following questions

1. Describe what is meant by the term physical variables, and discuss three ways of controlling them in an experiment.

2. Explain the term demand characteristics, and discuss the research conducted by Orne and Scheibe (1964) in which demand characteristics were manipulated.

3. Explain the "good subject" phenomenon.

4. Discuss the two techniques for reducing demand characteristics in an experiment.

5. Explain what we mean by experimenter bias, and discuss how it can be controlled in an experiment.

6. Discuss the effects that can be produced by personality variables.

√ EXERCISES AND APPLICATIONS

1. Past research has shown that a number of personality characteristics of experimenters can influence how subjects perform in experiments. The kinds of effects produced by personality variables will vary in different kinds of experiments. So will the seriousness of the problem. Let's look at two examples:

(a) Jay and John are conducting an experiment to test the effects of room temperature on learning a list of 10 nonsense words. Jay is naturally a warm and friendly person, and his subjects respond positively to him. Their performance is high. John is a rather cold and aloof person. John's subjects do not react positively to him and their performance suffers. Below are the scores of 10 of Jay's subjects and 10 of John's (5 from each experimental condition).

	Jay			John	
	Warm room	Cold room		Warm room	Cold room
	8	7		6	5
	9	8		5	4
	7	6		4	3
	9	7		5	5
	8	6		6	4
Averages	8.2	6.8		5.2	4.2
Differences		1.4			1.0

Jay's subjects performed better overall, but the differences between the two experimental conditions was about the same; on average, subjects learned about one more word in the warm room than they did in the cold room.

(b) Suppose that Jay and John conducted a second experiment. This time Jay ran all the warm room subjects and John ran all the cold room subjects. Examine the new scores:

	Jay			John	
	Warm room	Warm room		Cold room	Cold room
	8	7		5	5
	9	8		5	4
	7	8		3	3
	9	9		4	5
	8	8		3	4

(The second part of the exercise continues on the next page.)

Calculate the average difference between the two experimental conditions in the second experiment.

Average for Warm room   _____

Average for Cold room   _____

Difference   _____

Notice how much larger the difference became. On average, subjects in the warm room learned four more words than subjects in the cold room did.

Answer the following questions:

   (c) The experimenters are clearly extraneous variables in this experiment. In the first experiment, their influence was distributed across all conditions of the experiment. This is like the control procedure called _____ . (p. 189)

   (d) In the second experiment, the experimenters changed systematically along with the independent variable. Thus, the second experiment was _____ . (p. 190)

   (e) The second experiment has the more serious problem. Why is the problem more serious?

√ RESEARCH IDEAS

1. Plan to conduct a simple between-subjects experiment on list learning. Your hypothesis is that pronounceable letter pairs will be easier to memorize than nonpronounceable pairs. Your dependent variable will be the time it takes each subject to memorize the list. Plan on five subjects per condition.

    (a) You will need to create two sets of letter pairs: one that contains 10 letter pairs that are pronounceable, such as *er* and *il*, and another set that contains unpronounceable pairs, such as *gb* and *dk*.

    List 1 (pronounceable)   List 2 (unpronounceable)

1.	6.	1.	6.
2.	7.	2.	7.
3.	8.	3.	8.
4.	9.	4.	9.
5.	10.	5.	10.

    Even a simple experiment like this requires control over a number of extraneous variables.

    (b) You will need to prepare a set of instructions to subjects. (Would you want to tell them the experimental hypothesis or what condition they are in? Probably not.) Create a **simple** set of instructions that could be read to subjects in both conditions:

    (c) What are you going to tell your subjects at the end of the experiment that you did not tell them up front?

(The experiment continues on the next page.)

(d) How are you going to deal with the problem of experimenter bias?

(e) What physical variables will you need to control, and how will you do it?

(f) How will you select subjects and assign them to conditions?

(g) How will you order the word pairs for the five subjects in each condition?

(h) How will you measure and record each person's time?

Times

List 1 (pronounceable)	List 2 (unpronounceable)
1.	1.
2.	2.
3.	3.
4.	4.
5.	5.

Averages _____   _____

(i) Did the data appear to support your hypothesis?

(j) Any problems?

ANSWERS TO FILL-IN AND MULTIPLE CHOICE QUESTIONS

Fill-in

1. physical (187)
2. constancy of conditions (188)
3. balancing (189)
4. social (191)
5. demand characteristics (191)
6. good subject (193)
7. single-blind (195)
8. placebo (196)
9. cover story (197)
10. experimenter bias (198)
11. experimenter bias (198)
12. Rosenthal (199)
13. double-blind (202)
14. personality (204)
15. authoritarian (205)
16. context (206)
17. selecting; assigning (207)

Multiple choice

1. c (187)
2. b (188)
3. c (188)
4. a (188)
5. c (191)
6. b (191)
7. d (193)
8. a (194)
9. a (195)
10. b (196)
11. d (197)
12. c (197)
13. a (199)
14. b (199)
15. a (202)
16. d (204)
17. d (205)

SUGGESTED READINGS

Jung, J. (1971). *The experimenter's dilemma.* New York: Harper & Row.

Rosenthal, R., & Rosnow, R. L (1969). *Artifact in behavioral research.* New York: Academic Press.

8 CHAPTER EIGHT
Basic Between-Subjects Designs

Chapter Outline

√√ CHAPTER OBJECTIVES: KEY CONCEPTS

Listed below are questions that test the major concepts you should know from Chapter 8. After reading the chapter, you should be able to answer each of the questions below. If not, go back to the book and read the appropriate sections again before continuing on in the Study Guide.

----

1. What is an <u>experimental design</u>? A <u>between-subjects design</u>? (213)

2. What are the approaches suggested in the text for <u>selecting and recruiting subjects</u>? (214)

3. Can you explain why <u>large samples</u> are better than <u>small samples</u>? (215)

4. What is effect size, and how is it related to the number of subjects? (217)

5. How is <u>random assignment</u> used in a two independent groups design, and why is it important? (218)

6. What is an <u>experimental group-control group design</u>? How does a no treatment condition differ from a true control condition? (221)

7.   Explain the <u>two experimental groups design</u>. (224)

8.   Describe the <u>two matched groups design</u>. When is it used? (229, 231)

9.   Describe the three <u>matching procedures</u> (precision, range, and rank-ordered) discussed in the text. (230)

10.   What is a <u>multiple groups design</u>, and when is it used? (233)

11.   What does block randomization accomplish? (234)

12.   Describe the important factors to consider in choosing the <u>number of treatments</u> and what they will be. (236)

13.   What are the <u>practical limits</u> to consider in multiple groups experiments? (239)

KEY TERMS: *define each term using your own words*

Experimental design (213):

Between-subjects designs (213):

Effect size (217):

Two group design (217):

Two independent groups design (218):

Random assignment (218):

Experimental group-control group design (221):

Experimental condition (221):

Experimental group (221):

Control condition (221):

Control group (221):

Placebo group (223):

Two experimental groups design (224):

Two matched groups design (229):

Precision matching (230):

Range matching (230):

Rank-ordered matching (231):

Multiple groups design (233):

Multiple independent groups design (233):

Block randomization (234):

Pilot study (239):

149

√ QUESTIONS FOR REVIEW AND STUDY

FILL INS: *fill in the blanks with the right word or phrase*

1. The experimental design is the general _____ of the experiment--not its specific _____.

2. In _____ designs, each subject takes part in only one condition of the experiment.

3. From a statistical standpoint, an experiment has less power to detect effects with _____ samples.

4. Even if a researcher cannot use random selection, he or she must use random _____ to treatment conditions.

5. Very often, control conditions involve carefully arranging for conditions that _____ for what control group subjects are doing.

6. A between-subjects experiment to test whether highly violent music videos would produce more aggressiveness than music videos with low violence would use a _____ design.

7. When random assignment is successful, the treatment groups are said to be _____; although they are not identical.

8. When researchers are worried that random assignment might not result in groups that are comparable on an important extraneous variable that might produce confounding, they sometimes use _____ procedures.

9. _____ matching is more commonly used than
   _____ matching.

10. When independent groups are used, we must combine, or
    _____, the data from each group and compare group averages.

11. Matching is more useful when the number of subjects is _____.

12. When more than two treatment conditions are needed to make a good
    test of the hypothesis, researchers can use a
    _____ design.

13. When randomly assigning subjects to several treatment conditions,
    researchers can use the random number table or the procedure called
    _____.

14. Because different values of the same _____
    variable can produce different effects, researchers often test more than
    two levels of an _____ variable.

15. The three distances used in Lassen's experiment were dictated by
    _____.

16. When selecting levels of an independent variable, they should be
    extreme enough to bring out differences; however, they also should be
    _____.

17. A mini-experiment to test the appropriateness of the selected levels is
    called a _____ .

*Correct answers are located at the end of the chapter, but do not
look at them until you have completed the test.*

√ QUESTIONS FOR REVIEW AND STUDY

MULTIPLE CHOICE: *circle the best answer to each question*

1. Which of the following is <u>not</u> an important aspect in determining a research design?
   a. the number of dependent variables
   b. the number of independent variables
   c. the number of treatment conditions needed
   d. whether the same or different subjects receive each treatment

2. Which of the following was suggested by Rosnow and Rosenthal (1976) to aid in recruiting subjects?
   a. Ask your friends to be subjects in the experiment.
   b. Have a stranger from their peer group ask them.
   c. Give subjects a small gift for listening.
   d. Give the experiment an interesting title.

3. When individuals in the population are very similar on the DV, it is okay to use _____ samples.
   a. nonrepresentative
   b. convenience
   c. average
   d. small

4. Statistics are used to decide whether differences in treatment effects are _____ .
   a. detectable
   b. significant
   c. powerful
   d. meaningful

5. The simplest experiments test the effects of _____ .
   a. a single subject
   b. a small number of subjects
   c. one independent variable
   d. one dependent variable

6.   If subjects are <u>not</u> selected at random, the experiment will have less
     _____ .
     a. internal validity
     b. external validity
     c. power
     d. control

7.   Assigning subjects at random _____ .
     a. controls for preexisting differences among subjects
     b. keeps the experiment free from confounding
     c. is critical to an experiment's external validity
     d. controls for what subjects are doing in each condition

8.   _____ produced confounding in Brady's experiment to study ulcers in
     executive monkeys.
     a. Sacrificing the executive but not the control monkeys for study
     b. Creating a situation where one condition was more stressful than
        another
     c. Allowing only the executive monkeys to control shock
     d. Failure to randomly assign monkeys to different conditions

9.   An experimental condition in which nothing happens to subjects is
     called a _____ condition.
     a. no treatment
     b. comparison
     c. manipulation
     d. measurement

10. In psychotherapy research, the control group is often a(n) _____
     control group.
     a. placebo
     b. no treatment
     c. waiting-list
     d. expected-benefits

11. Holloway and Hornstein's (1976) research testing good vs. bad news
     used a(n) _____ design.
     a. experimental group-control group
     b. two experimental groups
     c. two matched groups
     d. multiple groups

12. To test the hypothesis that 15 minutes of exercise is better than 10 minutes would require a(n) _____ design.
    a. experimental group-control group
    b. two experimental groups
    c. two matched groups
    d. multiple groups

13. We could test the hypothesis that cockroaches will run faster in the presence of an audience than when they are alone using a(n) _____ design.
    a. experimental group-control group
    b. two experimental groups
    c. two matched groups
    d. multiple groups

14. Which of the following is not true of a matched-groups design?
    a. Subjects are measured on the extraneous variable used for matching.
    b. Pairs of subjects are formed from identical or close scores on the matching variable.
    c. Members of each pair of subjects are randomly assigned to treatments.
    d. Matching on a variable not strongly related to the DV makes it easier to detect effects that may be present.

15. A multiple groups design is often preferred to a two groups design because it _____ .
    a. allows more control over extraneous variables
    b. tests more than one hypothesis in the same experiment
    c. provides a better understanding of how the IV operates
    d. maximizes the possibility of seeing changes across conditions

16. Which of the following is not true of multiple groups experiments?
    a. Subjects are assigned randomly to each treatment condition.
    b. There are as many treatment groups as there are levels of the IV.
    c. It uses many fewer subjects than a two groups experiment.
    d. It allows us to compare the behavior of different groups of subjects.

Correct answers are located at the end of the chapter, but do not look at them until you have completed the test.

√ QUESTIONS FOR REVIEW AND STUDY

SHORT ESSAY: *use the information in the chapter to answer the following questions*

---

1.   Discuss how the selection and size of your sample can affect external validity.

2.   Describe the two independent groups design, and discuss the purpose of random assignment to each of the two conditions. (Use an experimental example to illustrate what you mean.)

3.   Explain the experimental group-control group design, and discuss what a control group is used for. (Use an experimental example to illustrate what you mean.)

4.   Explain the two matched groups design. Why do we sometimes match subjects? How is matching done?

5.	What is a multiple groups experiment, and why is it used? What are the practical considerations that influence the choice of this design?

6.	How does a researcher determine what kind of design to use?

√ EXERCISES AND APPLICATIONS

1. Imagine that you are a researcher who is interested in comparing two different "reading readiness" programs (A and B) designed to give preschoolers a head start toward learning to read when they begin kindergarten. The Tiny Tots 'n Toddlers preschool in your neighborhood has offered to let you conduct your experiment using the thirty 4-year-olds who currently attend preschool every day as your subjects (with the parents' consent and the children's agreement). You need to decide on a research design. Several between-subjects research designs are possible: (a) a two experimental groups design; (b) a two matched* groups design; (c) a multiple groups design that includes a control condition; (d) a multiple groups design with matched subjects.

   (a) Briefly describe each treatment condition in the experiment that could result from each of the four designs.

Two experimental groups design:

Two matched groups design:

Multiple groups design (including a control group):

Multiple groups design (including a control group) with matched subjects:

*Assume that you discovered that researchers in about half of the prior studies on children's reading skills have matched subjects on their IQ's.

(The second part of the exercise continues on the next page.)

(b) Some research psychologists do not like to use matching. They believe that "matching always undermatches." When we match subjects on some characteristic, such as IQ, it is because we believe the characteristic is a factor that is very important in determining how subjects will score on the dependent variable. If other important factors exist, however, matching on one characteristic can sometimes work against detecting significant differences between treatment conditions. It is not always easy to know what matching variable to use. To give you an idea of the problem, think about the many biological, social, cultural, and psychological factors that might influence a young child's reading skills. List as many as you can in the space below. To get you started, a few items are already listed.

1. IQ
2. Visual skills
3. Language spoken at home
4. Nutrition
5. Number of storybooks

1. Researchers studying music videos have discovered that liking for music videos with explicit sexual themes is influenced by a number of personal characteristics, such as gender, age, and how much time people spend watching them on TV. Imagine that you wanted to conduct a two group experiment to compare the effects of sexual and nonsexual music videos on the positivity of people's moods. To control for factors such as the performer, the type of music, etc., you will show subjects different videos from Ricky Martin: each subject will see two videos with sexual themes or two videos with nonsexual themes. Then you will ask them to rate how they feel on the following scale:

Very Unhappy   Neutral   Very Happy
      0   1   2   3   4   5   6   7   8

Before you can conduct the experiment, though, you need to decide whether to use a two independent groups design or a two matched groups design. To control for gender and age effects, you do not need to match subjects. Instead, you could use subjects of one gender (say, male) who were all approximately the same age (18-19). You decide to match 32 subjects on the remaining variable, how much time they watch music videos (<1 hour per week = seldom watch; >1 hour per week = frequently watch*). Using a coin flip, you randomly assign one member of each pair to the sexual or neutral condition; the other pair member goes in the unchosen condition. Below are the scores of the 32 matched young men:

Sexual Videos		Nonsexual Videos	
F1 = 8	F2 = 7	F1 = 5	F2 = 6
F3 = 7	F4 = 6	F3 = 4	F4 = 5
F5 = 4	F6 = 6	F5 = 5	F6 = 7
F7 = 5	F8 = 8	F7 = 4	F8 = 5
S1 = 2	S2 = 2	S1 = 6	S2 = 3
S3 = 3	S4 = 3	S3 = 5	S4 = 6
S5 = 1	S6 = 4	S5 = 4	S6 = 4
S7 = 3	S8 = 3	S7 = 4	S8 = 7

*The letter "S" designates a subject who watches seldom; the letter "F" designates a frequent watcher.

(The second part of the experiment continues on the next page.)

(a) Calculate the average score for each condition. Which type of video seemed to produce the most positive mood?

Average _____   Average _____

(b) Now, see what would have happened if the subjects had not been matched. Using a coin, make heads = sexual videos, and tails = nonsexual videos. Go through each of the 32 subjects, and imagine you were randomly assigning each of the young men to one of the two video conditions. Count how many F's and S's fell into each condition by random assignment.

	Sexual Videos	Nonsexual Videos
Number of F's		
Number of S's		

How well did random assignment by coin flip work in terms of balancing the number of F's and S's in each group?

(c) Now, assign each of the 32 subjects a number from 1 to 32. Using the random number table at the back of your text, locate a series of 10 numbers from 1 to 32, and write them below.

___ ___ ___ ___ ___ ___ ___ ___ ___ ___

Using the subjects that correspond to each number you located, use a coin to randomly assign all 10 subjects to one of the two groups. Count how many F's and S's fell into each condition by random assignment.

	Sexual Videos	Nonsexual Videos
Number of F's		
Number of S's		

How well did random assignment work in terms of balancing the number of F's and S's in each group?

According to Bernoulli's law (text, p. 201), your groups should have been more balanced in terms of F's and S's when you randomly assigned 32 subjects than when you randomly assigned 10. What does this tell you about the relationship between the number of available subjects and matching?

ANSWERS TO FILL-IN AND MULTIPLE CHOICE QUESTIONS

Fill-in

1. structure; content (213)
2. between-subjects (213)
3. smaller (216)
4. assignment (218)
5. control (222)
6. two experimental groups (224)
7. equivalent (226)
8. matching (229)
9. range; precision (230)
10. pool (232)
11. small (232)
12. multiple groups (233)
13. block randomization (234)
14. independent; independent (236)
15. prior research (237)
16. realistic (239)
17. pilot study (239)

Multiple choice

1. a (213)
2. c (214)
3. d (216)
4. b (216)
5. c (217)
6. b (218)
7. a (218)
8. d (220)
9. a (221)
10. c (223)
11. b (224)
12. b (224)
13. b (226)
14. d (232)
15. c (236)
16. c (239)

SUGGESTED READINGS

Greeson, L. E. (1991). Recognition and ratings of television music videos: Age, gender, and sociocultural effects. *Journal of Applied Social Psychology, 21,* 1908-1920.

Toney, G. T., & Weaver, J. B. (1994). Effects of gender and gender role self-perceptions on affective reactions to rock music videos. *Sex Roles, 30,* 567-583.

⑨ C H A P T E R   N I N E
Between-Subjects Factorial Designs

Chapter Outline

√√ CHAPTER OBJECTIVES: KEY CONCEPTS

Listed below are questions that test the major concepts you should know from Chapter 9. After reading the chapter, you should be able to answer each of the questions below. If not, go back to the book and read the appropriate sections again before continuing on in the Study Guide.

_____

1. What is a <u>factorial design</u>? Why is it an efficient approach to experimentation? (245)

2. What are <u>main effects</u>? How many are there in an experiment? (246)

3. What is an <u>interaction</u>? How many are there in an experiment? What is a <u>higher-order interaction</u>? (247)

4. Diagram the 2 x 2 experiment in <u>Box 9-1</u>. (249)

5. How is a factorial design diagrammed in a <u>design matrix</u>? (250)

6. What do we mean by shorthand notation? What are the different methods for describing the variables in a factorial experiment? (251)

7. Explain the procedures used and the effects found in the Pliner and Chaiken (1990) experiment. (253)

8. Do you understand how to interpret each of the graphs shown in Figures 9-5 through 9-11? (256)

9. Describe the three types of interactions (divergent, convergent, and intersecting [or crossover]). (257)

10. Why do we say that when an interaction is present, we cannot predict effects unless we know a subject's position on each factor? (258)

11. Describe the important considerations in choosing a between-subjects design. (259)

12. What interactions were found by Baron and his colleagues? (262)

√ QUESTIONS FOR REVIEW AND STUDY

KEY TERMS: *define each term using your own words*

Factorial design (246):

Factor (246):

Two factor experiment (246):

Main effect (246):

Interaction (247):

Higher-order interaction (247):

Shorthand notation (251):

√ QUESTIONS FOR REVIEW AND STUDY

FILL INS: *fill in the blanks with the right word or phrase*

_____

1. To test more than one independent variable in the same experiment, we use a(n) _____ design.

2. A(n) _____ is the effect of a single factor in a factorial experiment.

3. When the effects of one factor change across the levels of another, a(n) _____ is present.

4. _____ interactions involve more than two factors at the same time.

5. Main effects and interactions are measured quantitatively using _____ .

6. We can look at a factorial design graphically if we diagram it using a(n) _____ .

7. In the Mehrabian and Piercy (1993a) experiment, nicknames were judged warmer, friendlier, and more _____ than given first names.

8. Factorial designs can be described using numbers; this is called _____.

9. Variables are named in the factor-labeling methods and the _____ methods.

167

10. A 2 x 3 x 2 factorial design has _____ (how many?) conditions.

11. In the Pliner and Chaiken (1990) experiment on eating behavior, eating was measured by counting the number of _____ eaten.

12. The maximum interaction possible in a factorial experiment is called a(n) _____ interaction.

13. In a factorial experiment, an interaction can occur along with any number of significant _____.

14. When an interaction is present, precise effects cannot be predicted without knowing the levels of both _____.

15. A review of the experimental _____ can help you decide what variables to include in your experiment.

16. A significant _____ interaction is rarely a predicted result, and _____ interactions are practically impossible to conceptualize and explain.

17. The design of an experiment is largely determined by the number of independent variables and the number of _____ conditions need to test the hypothesis.

18. The results of the negative ion experiment were difficult to interpret because two significant _____ interactions were obtained.

Correct answers are located at the end of the chapter, but do not look at them until you have completed the test.

√ QUESTIONS FOR REVIEW AND STUDY

MULTIPLE CHOICE: circle the best answer to each question

1. Which of the following is <u>not</u> an advantage of using a factorial design?
    a. It is more efficient.
    b. It tests for the presence of interactions.
    c. It uses fewer subjects.
    d. It tests for the separate effects of each factor.

2. In a factorial experiment, there are as many main effects as _____ .
    a. factors
    b. variables
    c. interactions
    d. levels

3. Statistics are used to tell us whether effects from a factorial experiment are _____.
    a. main effects
    b. meaningful
    c. factorial
    d. significant

4. Which of the following describes an interaction?
    a. Plants that get watered do not grow any faster with music.
    b. Both water and music improve plant growth.
    c. Music affects plant growth more than water.
    d. Water affects plant growth, but music does not.

5. An interaction between water, music, and speech would be called a _____ interaction.
    a. multiple effects
    b. higher-order
    c. significant
    d. three variable

6. Average group ratings for the _____ can be recorded in the matrix.
    a. main effects
    b. interaction
    c. factors
    d. dependent variable

7. A design matrix for a 2 x 2 experiment would have four _____ .
   a. factors
   b. values
   c. cells
   d. variables

8. Describing the experiment to test the type of name and name length as a 2 x 2 factorial is an example of _____.
   a. a design matrix
   b. shorthand notation
   c. the factor and levels method
   d. the factor-labeling method

9. In a 2 x 3 x 2 experiment, there are _____ factors.
   a. 2
   b. 3
   c. 5
   d. 12

10. How many separate treatment conditions would there be in the experiment in question 9?
    a. 3
    b. 5
    c. 6
    d. 12

11. The independent variables in the Pliner and Chaiken (1990) research example were _____ .
    a. sex and eating behavior
    b. subject sex and type of partner
    c. partner sex and eating behavior
    d. subject sex, partner sex, and eating behavior

12. Which of the following was not among Pliner and Chaiken's (1990) results?
    a. Overall, women ate less than men.
    b. Men ate about the same amount whether their partner was the same or the opposite sex.
    c. Men ate more in the presence of a same-sex partner than an opposite-sex partner.
    d. Women varied their eating depending on the gender of their partner.

13. A graph of the interaction found by Pliner and Chaiken (1990) showed
_____ .
   a. two intersecting lines
   b. two parallel lines
   c. two lines that diverged
   d. two lines that converged

14. When the effects of factor 1 completely reverse at each level of factor 2,
a _____ is present.
   a. main effect
   b. main effect and an interaction
   c. crossover interaction
   d. divergent interaction

15. In the experiment by Aronson et al. (1999) in Box 9-3, there was a
crossover interaction between _____ .
   a. gender and math performance
   b. race and gender
   c. math identification and stereotype threat
   d. math abilities and stereotype threat

16. Which of the following is not one of the reasons given for keeping
factorial designs simple?
   a. More factors mean more time is needed to run the experiment.
   b. Higher-order interactions are very difficult to explain.
   c. Complex designs take more time to analyze with statistics.
   d. The more complex the design, the more extraneous variables you
   will need to control.

17. Which of the following effects, depicted in the graph in Box 9-4, was
found by Baron and his colleagues (1985)?
   a. Increasing the level of negative ions increased the aggressiveness
   of Type A subjects.
   b. Type A subjects were more aggressive at lower levels of negative
   ions than Type B subjects.
   c. Type B subjects were more aggressive at all levels of negative ions
   than Indeterminate subjects.
   d. Type A subjects were less aggressive than the other two groups at
   moderate levels of negative ions.

**Correct answers are located at the end of the chapter, but do not
look at them until you have completed the test.**

√ QUESTIONS FOR REVIEW AND STUDY

SHORT ESSAY: use the information in the chapter to answer the following questions

_____

1. Discuss how a factorial experiment can have advantages over conducting separate experiments testing one independent variable at a time.

2. What do we mean by the term main effects? Interaction? (Use an experimental example to illustrate what you mean.)

3.   Describe the use of a design matrix. Illustrate your answer by drawing a design matrix for the stereotype study by Aronson et al. (1999) in Box 9-3.

4.   Explain shorthand notation. Describe the stereotype threat experiment from question 3 in shorthand notation, and, using each of the four methods in Box 9-2, label the variables.

5. Discuss the Pliner and Chaiken (1990) experiment on eating behavior. What procedures were used in the experiment? What were the variables tested? What effects were found?

6. Use an experimental example to explain how a significant interaction "qualifies" significant main effects in a factorial experiment.

√ EXERCISES AND APPLICATIONS

1. Return to the exercise on "reading readiness" programs from the last chapter. Suppose that you wanted to conduct a factorial experiment testing the two reading programs (A and B). Prior research, however, has suggested that 4-year-old girls might be more skilled in verbal tasks than 4-year-old boys, so you want to use the child's gender as a second factor. This time your subjects are forty 4-year-olds (20 boys and 20 girls) from the Tiny Tots 'n Toddlers preschool.

(a) Using shorthand notation, describe the design of your experiment. Label the variables using the first of the factor and levels methods described in Box 9-2.

(b) Diagram the experiment using a design matrix:

(The second part of the exercise continues on the next page.)

(c) Now, suppose you decided to add another factor: IQ. You measured each child's IQ and then grouped each child in one of three categories: low, average, or high IQ. In shorthand notation, your experiment is now a 2 x 2 x 3 factorial. Use the first factor and levels method to write out the complete, labeled design:

(d) Using Figure 9-3 from Chapter 9 as a guide, diagram the design below:

√ RESEARCH IDEAS

1. Now that you are familiar with the material in Chapter 9, you can design a more sophisticated study of music videos than the one from last chapter's Research Ideas. Instead of matching subjects on the amount of time they watch music videos, you can separate subjects into either F (frequently watch) or S (seldom watch) groups and take that variable as a factor in the design. You can also expand the design to include female as well as male subjects by taking gender as an additional factor. Your design will now have three factors: type of video shown, prior amount of viewing, and gender.

    (a) Describe the full design using shorthand notation and the first factor-labeling method:

    (b) Below is a design matrix for this study. Mean mood scale scores for subjects in each treatment condition are shown in the cells.

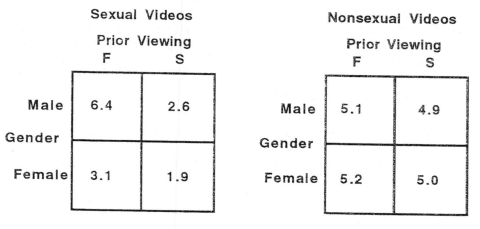

(Continued on the next page.)

(c) Look at the right half of the diagram. Everyone's scores are remarkably similar, suggesting that men and women felt moderately happy after the nonsexual videos regardless of their prior viewing history. Now look at the left half: sexual videos. The scores are very different in the four cells. Use these numbers to answer the following questions:

What was the average score for all the men in the experiment? _____
  (average = sum of [6.4 + 2.6 + 5.1 + 4.9]; divided by 4)

What was the average score for all the women in the experiment? _____

Which gender was happier, overall, after watching videos? _____

(d) The effects were actually quite different for sexual and nonsexual videos. For the nonsexual videos, gender did not make much difference overall (5.0 for men vs. 5.1 for women). But, what happened with sexual videos?

What was the men's average score for sexual videos? _____

What was the women's average score for sexual videos? _____

Did gender seem to make a difference for the sexual videos? _____

(e) For the nonsexual videos, prior viewing did not matter very much (5.15 for F's vs. 4.95 for S's). But, what happened with sexual videos?

What was the F's average score for sexual videos? _____

What was the S's average score for sexual videos? _____

Did prior viewing seem to make a difference for the sexual videos? _____

(Continued on the next page.)

178

(f) The four cells from the nonsexual video condition are graphed
   below:

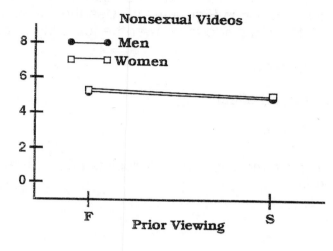

(g) Graph the four cells from the sexual video condition below:

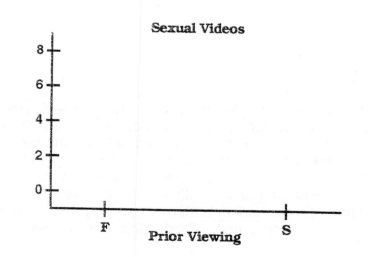

(Continued on the next page.)

179

(h) Look at what the two graphs tell you about differences produced by the two types of videos. The graph of the cells in the nonsexual video conditions is much like Figure 9-5 from Chapter 9. In the nonsexual video conditions, neither gender nor prior viewing had an effect on people's moods.

But, the graph of the sexual video conditions shows effects that are most similar to those in Figure 9-11.   Use the explanation of effects in Figure 9-11 as a guide to answer the following questions:

Does gender have an effect? _____

Does prior viewing have an effect? _____

Do the two factors interact? _____

   (i) In words, explain the set of effects depicted in the graph of the sexual video conditions:

(j) The effects of both gender and prior viewing differed across the levels of the other factor, type of video. In other words, in this experiment all three factors interacted, making the full set of effects difficult to explain. Breaking down all of the effects given in the design matrix by graphing the effects separately for the nonsexual and sexual video conditions allows you to visualize the three-factor interaction. By explaining both of these graphs, you have explained the three factor interaction! What is this kind of complex interaction called?   _____

180

ANSWERS TO FILL-IN AND MULTIPLE CHOICE QUESTIONS

Fill-in

1. factorial (246)
2. main effect (246)
3. interaction (247)
4. Higher-order (247)
5. statistical tests (248)
6. design matrix (248)
7. popular (249)
8. shorthand notation (251)
9. factor and levels (252)
10. 12 (253)
11. crackers (254)
12. crossover (257)
13. main effects (257)
14. factors (258)
15. literature (259)
16. 3-way; 4-way (261)
17. treatment (261)
18. 2-way (262)

Multiple choice

1. c (245)
2. a (246)
3. d (246)
4. a (246)
5. b (247)
6. d (248)
7. c (250)
8. b (251)
9. b (251)
10. d (253)
11. b (254)
12. c (255)
13. a (256)
14. c (257)
15. c (260)
16. d (261)
17. a (263)

SUGGESTED READINGS

Salkind, N. J. (2000). *Statistics for people who (think they) hate statistics.* Thousand Oaks, CA: Sage Publications.

Runyon, R. P., Coleman, K. A., & Pittenger, D. J. (2000). *Fundamentals of behavioral statistics* (9th ed.). Boston: McGraw Hill.

10 C H A P T E R   T E N
Within-Subjects Designs

Chapter Outline

√√ CHAPTER OBJECTIVES: KEY CONCEPTS

Listed below are questions that test the major concepts you should know from Chapter 10. After reading the chapter, you should be able to answer each of the questions below. If not, go back to the book and read the appropriate sections again before continuing on in the Study Guide.

---

1. Why is it preferable to use a <u>within-subjects design</u> when responses from subjects are expected to be extremely dissimilar? (270)

2. Describe the experiment by <u>McBeath and his colleagues</u>. Why did they select a within-subjects design? (272)

3. Describe a <u>within-subjects factorial design</u>, and give an example. (272)

4. Describe a <u>mixed design</u>, and give an example. (273)

5. What are the <u>advantages</u> and <u>disadvantages</u> of a within-subjects design? (274, 276)

6. Can you describe <u>interference</u> between conditions and give an example? (277)

183

7. What are <u>order effects</u>? How can order effects confound a within-subjects experiment? (278)

8. Explain <u>progressive error</u>, and describe <u>fatigue</u> and <u>practice effects</u>. (279)

9. Explain the differences between <u>subject-by-subject</u> and <u>across-subjects counterbalancing</u>. (280, 282)

10. Explain the differences between <u>complete</u> and <u>partial counterbalancing</u>, and describe each of the partial counterbalancing techniques described in the text. (283, 285)

11. What is a <u>carryover effect</u>, and how can it be controlled? (286)

12. Why might we want to take <u>order as a factor</u> in the design? (290)

√ QUESTIONS FOR REVIEW AND STUDY

KEY TERMS: *define each term using your own words*

Within-subjects design (270):

Power (270):

Repeated-measures design (270):

Within-subjects factorial design (272):

Mixed design (273):

Order effects (278):

Fatigue effects (279):

Practice effects (279):

Progressive error (279):

Counterbalancing (280):

Subject-by-subject counterbalancing (280):

Reverse counterbalancing (281):

Block randomization (282):

186

Across-subjects counterbalancing (283):

Complete counterbalancing (283):

Partial counterbalancing (285):

Randomized counterbalancing (285):

Latin square counterbalancing (285):

Carryover effects (286):

Balanced Latin square (287):

187

√ QUESTIONS FOR REVIEW AND STUDY

FILL INS: fill in the blanks with the right word or phrase

1. When subjects' responses are very dissimilar, researchers may prefer to use a(n) _____ design.

2. A within-subjects design is also known as a(n) _____ design.

3. In a within-subjects design there is better control over _____ variables.

4. An experiment that showed each subject pictures of four different facial expressions posed by both men and women would be using a within-subjects _____ design.

5. An experiment that combines both within- and between-subjects independent variables is called a(n) _____ design.

6. In a sense, the within-subjects design is the most perfect form of _____.

7. When the use of one condition makes the use of another condition impossible, the problem is called _____.

8. When performance is always better in the first condition of an experiment, the problem is known as a(n) _____ effect.

9. Fatigue effects and practice effects are both components of _____ error.

10. Several _____ procedures are available to control for order effects in within-subjects experiments.

11. The procedure that presents each possible order sequence an equal number of times to different subjects is called _____ counterbalancing.

12. To tell how many sequences are needed for complete counterbalancing with six conditions, compute 6 _____ .

13. We are using a procedure called _____ partial counterbalancing when we select as many chance order sequences as we have subjects.

14. As a general rule, the minimum number of order sequences used in an experiment is equal to the number of _____ conditions.

15. When effects of a treatment condition persist after the treatment is removed, a _____ effect is present.

16. To know whether partial counterbalancing is successful, an experimenter can consider using order as a design _____ .

Correct answers are located at the end of the chapter, but do not look at them until you have completed the test.

√ QUESTIONS FOR REVIEW AND STUDY

MULTIPLE CHOICE: circle the best answer to each question

1. From a statistical viewpoint, increased power means _____ .
   a. a greater chance of detecting an effect of the independent variable
   b. using fewer subjects for a longer time instead of many subjects for a short time
   c. greater external validity from effects with many fewer subjects
   d. detecting effects with fewer treatment conditions

2. What were the results of the experiment by McBeath and his colleagues?
   a. The direction a figure seemed to face caused a perceptual bias.
   b. The most forward-facing errors occurred with the letter R.
   c. Figures facing forward were perceived as moving faster than figures facing backward.
   d. Circular figures produced a stronger forward-facing bias than squares or triangles.

3. An experiment in which each subject was asked to evaluate three kinds of kitchen appliances in both white and almond colors would be a _____ design.
   a. 3 X 2 mixed
   b. multiple groups
   c. 3 X 2 within-subjects factorial
   d. 2 X 2 repeated measures

4. An experiment comparing preferences of men and women for soft rock, hard rock, and alternative music would use a _____ design.
   a. 2 X 3 mixed
   b. multiple-groups
   c. 2 X 2 repeated measures
   d. 2 X 3 within-subjects factorial

5. Which of the following is <u>not</u> true of within-subjects designs?
   a. They use fewer subjects.
   b. The sessions take less time.
   c. They exert greater control over extraneous variables.
   d. They improve the chances of detecting a treatment effect.

6. Using a within-subjects design, Niedenthal and Setterlund found that
   _____ .
   a. a good mood made a list of positive words easier to identify
   b. good or bad moods influenced subjects' ability to detect words in a similar category
   c. happy subjects were faster at identifying happy words; sad subjects did better with sad words
   d. more of the strings of letters were identified as words than as nonwords by happy subjects

7. Which of the following is a potential disadvantage of using a within-subjects design?
   a. Experimental sessions can become long and tedious.
   b. A within-subjects design can be more easily confounded.
   c. Individual differences in subjects are not well controlled.
   d. Statistically, it is not as powerful as a between-subjects design.

8. Which of the following is not a potential disadvantage of using a within-subjects design?
   a. interference between conditions
   b. fugue effects
   c. order effects
   d. carryover effects

9. Which of the following is not a component of progressive error?
   a. order effects
   b. practice effects
   c. fatigue effects
   d. contrast effects

10. Which of the following counterbalancing procedures presents each condition to subjects more than once?
    a. Latin square
    b. across-subjects
    c. subject-by-subject
    d. complete

11. The effects of progressive error might be all of the following except
    _____ .
    a. linear
    b. extralinear
    c. nonmonotonic
    d. curvilinear

12. A subset of the available order sequences is presented to subjects in
    _____ counterbalancing.
    a. complete
    b. partial
    c. subject-by-subject
    d. across-subjects

13. When one treatment condition makes a subsequent condition easier or
    harder, the experiment is demonstrating a(n) _____ effect.
    a. carryover
    b. order
    c. persistence
    d. position

14. An experimenter designed a within-subjects experiment with four
    treatment conditions. To control for order, two different Latin squares
    were constructed. Which of the two squares below would provide the
    best control, and why?

A	B	C	D		A	B	C	D
B	A	D	C		B	D	A	C
C	D	A	B		C	A	D	B
D	C	B	A		D	C	B	A

    Square one   Square two

    a. Square one--each treatment appears only once in each position.
    b. Square one--the first and last rows are reverses of each other.
    c. Square two--it controls for both order and carryover effects.
    d. It doesn't matter; either is okay.

15. When one condition carries over more than another, a researcher
    should consider using _____ .
    a. order as a design factor
    b. several different random orders
    c. subject-by-subject counterbalancing
    d. a between-subjects design

16. Within-subjects designs are better from a(n) _____ standpoint.
    a. statistical
    b. theoretical
    c. practical
    d. empirical

**Correct answers are located at the end of the chapter, but do not
look at them until you have completed the test.**

√ QUESTIONS FOR REVIEW AND STUDY

1. Describe the three different kinds of designs in which subjects serve in more than one treatment condition of the experiment.

2. What are the advantages of using a within-subjects design?

3. What are the disadvantages of using a within-subjects design?

4. Explain what we mean by order effects in a within-subjects experiment, and give an example to illustrate what you mean.

5.   Explain what we mean by carryover effects, and give an example.

6.   Explain the various counterbalancing techniques.

√ EXERCISES AND APPLICATIONS

1. Imagine that you are planning to conduct a within-subjects experiment with four treatment conditions: A, B, C, and D. You will need to control the order in which the treatments are presented.

    (a) Calculate 4! to see how many order sequences are possible with four conditions.

    1 X 2 X 3 X 4 = _____

    (b) List all 24 order sequences.

    (c) Suppose you only had four subjects available. You will use partial counterbalancing, and you will need to create four different order sequences. You can use four different random orders, or you can create a Latin square. Try both techniques to see which one works best to control order effects.

My four random order sequences are:

My Latin square looks like this:

(The second part of the exercise continues on the next page.)

Use the sequences you created to answer the following questions:
(d) Which set of order sequences worked better? Why?

(e) Below is a balanced Latin square. Notice that no condition appears in any position more than once or precedes or follows another more than once. How do your sequences measure up?

A	B	C	D
B	D	A	C
C	A	D	B
D	C	B	A

(f) Assume that you are worried about carryover effects. If you could not obtain more than four subjects, what would you do?

(g) Suppose you had 24, rather than 4, subjects. How would you handle order and carryover effects?

√ **RESEARCH IDEAS**

1.   Conduct a very simple within-subjects experiment. Compare liking for two candy-coated chocolates: M&M's and a generic brand.

(a) Place three pieces of each type of candy in a small, covered paper cup. First, ask a volunteer if he or she would be willing to participate in a taste test of two kinds of chocolate candy. Once someone agrees, ask them to close their eyes and taste the M&M's (but don't tell them which candy they are tasting). After they are finished, have them rate the candy on the following scale:

How much did you like the candy you just tasted? (circle one number)
Not at all 0 1 2 3 4 5 6 7 8 9 Very much

Next, have them taste and rate the generic on the same scale.
Follow the same procedure until you have collected data from five subjects. Write their ratings below:

S#	M&M's	Generic	Difference
1			
2			
3			
4			
5			

Avg. Difference _____

Subtract each rating for the generic from the rating for the M&M's, and write the answer (+ or -) in the Difference column. Average the Differences.

(b) Now repeat the experiment with five new volunteers, switching the order of the two candies. Give them the generic first, then the M&M's. Record and calculate scores below (M&M's first):

S#	M&M's	Generic	Difference
1			
2			
3			
4			
5			

Avg. Difference _____

The second part of the experiment continues on the next page.)

Use your data* to answer the following questions:

      (c) Did your results show the same pattern of liking each time?

      (d) If not, what do you think caused the pattern to change?

      (e) To conduct this experiment properly, how would you control for order effects?

      (f) To conduct this experiment properly, how would you control for carryover effects?

      (g) What other extraneous variables would you need to control in order to conduct this experiment so that it would be free from confounding?

*A positive (+) average difference indicates greater liking, in general, for M&M's; a negative (-) average difference indicates greater liking for the generic.

ANSWERS TO FILL-IN AND MULTIPLE CHOICE QUESTIONS

Fill-in

1. within-subjects (270)
2. repeated-measures (270)
3. extraneous (270)
4. factorial (272)
5. mixed (273)
6. matching (276)
7. interference (277)
8. order (278)
9. progressive (279)
10. counterbalancing (280)
11. complete (283)
12. factorial (284)
13. randomized (285)
14. experimental (285)
15. carryover (286)
16. factor (291)

Multiple choice

1. a (270)
2. a (271)
3. c (272)
4. a (273)
5. b (274)
6. c (275)
7. a (276)
8. b (277)
9. d (279)
10. c (280)
11. b (282)
12. b (285)
13. a (286)
14. c (288)
15. d (291)
16. a (291)

SUGGESTED READINGS

Schweigert, W. A. (1994). *Research methods and statistics for psychology* (Chapter 8). Pacific Grove, CA: Brooks/Cole.

11 CHAPTER ELEVEN
Within-Subjects Designs: Small N

Chapter Outline

√√ CHAPTER OBJECTIVES: KEY CONCEPTS

Listed below are questions that test the major concepts you should know from Chapter 10. After reading the chapter, you should be able to answer each of the questions below. If not, go back to the book and read the appropriate sections again before continuing on in the Study Guide.

_____

1.   What is a <u>small N design</u>? When would we want to use it? Why would we want to use it? (298)

2.   Explain the small N experiment testing the <u>effect of talking on plant growth</u>. How was the effect of the independent variable verified in this *ABA* design? (301)

3.   Describe the <u>variations</u> on the basic *ABA* design. (303)

4.   Describe how an <u>*ABA* design</u> can be used with a large *N*. (304)

5.   What did <u>Miller and Kelley</u> (1994) do in their ABAB experiment? (306)

6.   What are the advantages and disadvantages of an _AB design_? (309)

7.   What is a multiple-baseline design, and when is it used? (309)

8.   Describe a discrete trials design. What makes it different from the _ABA_ family of small _N_ designs? (311)

9.   When would a researcher want to use a small _N_ design? (312)

10. How were pigeons trained to discriminate between paintings by Monet and Picasso? (313)

11. How is generalizability in a small N experiment related to the type of psychological process that is being investigated? (315)

√ QUESTIONS FOR REVIEW AND STUDY

KEY TERMS: *define each term using your own words*

Small *N* design (298):

Baseline (301):

ABA design (303):

ABABA design (303):

ABAB design (306):

AB design (309):

Multiple-baseline design (309):

Discrete trials design (311):

√ QUESTIONS FOR REVIEW AND STUDY

FILL INS: *fill in the blanks with the right word or phrase*

1. Researchers who prefer a small *N* design argue that large *N* designs lack _____ because they pool the data from many different subjects.

2. Before the 1930's, the _____ design predominated in psychology.

3. Small *N* designs are used most extensively today in experiments testing _____ conditioning.

4. A _____ is a measure of behavior as it normally occurs without the independent variable.

5. The small *N* experiment on the rubber plant used a(n) _____ design.

6. In the Pedalino and Gamboa (1974) study of workers' behavior, the independent variable was _____, and the dependent variable was _____.

7. An *ABACADA* design would present _____ (how many?) treatments to the same subject.

8. In clinical studies to modify self-injurious behavior, it might be unethical to return to the original _____ condition.

9. A psychologist who wanted to modify behavior that occurs in more than one setting could use a(n) _____ design.

10. The pattern of data obtained from a single subject may violate the assumptions behind many statistic tests unless _____ to _____ measurements are taken during each baseline and treatment period.

11. A(n) _____ design presents and averages across many applications of the treatment conditions instead of relying on comparisons between treatment conditions and baseline conditions.

12. A small N design is appropriate for studying a particular _____.

13. In the small N study by Watanabe and his colleagues (1995), reinforced pigeons averaged about _____ % correct discrimination between paintings by Monet and Picasso.

14. When we are measuring a process that is relatively invariant across people, a small N study would have more _____ than it would if the measured behavior showed large differences across people.

15. If we were conducting a small N study on a plant, and a cleaning person watered the plant on the night before we began a treatment, this would be considered a _____ threat to the internal validity of the experiment.

Correct answers are located at the end of the chapter, but do not look at them until you have completed the test.

QUESTIONS FOR REVIEW AND STUDY

MULTIPLE CHOICE: circle the best answer to each question

1. Small *N* designs are common in all of the following except _____ .
   a. clinical psychopathology research
   b. animal research
   c. psychophysics experiments
   d. social processes research

2. *ABA* designs are also known as _____ designs.
   a. small *N*
   b. reversal
   c. behaviorist
   d. multiple-baseline

3. In the large N design used by Pedalino and Gamboa (1974), it was essential to return to the nonreinforcement condition in order to rule out a(n) _____ threat.
   a. instrumentation
   b. maturation
   c. history
   d. statistical regression

4. Imagine that a psychologist used positive reinforcement to modify the eating behavior of an anorexic patient. As a result of the treatment, the patient began eating normally. According to Kazdin, what should the psychologist do now?
   a. Return to the baseline condition to verify that the reinforcement was producing the behavior change.
   b. Maintain the reinforcement, and return to the baseline condition.
   c. Change to an *ABAB* design.
   d. Maintain the reinforcement, and not return to the baseline condition.

5. Which of the following results were found in Miller and Kelley's (1994) experiment to improve homework performance?
   a. Performance was better during treatment than during baseline.
   b. Some improved with treatment, but others did not.
   c. Those with the most behavioral problems improved most.
   d. The second treatment was more effective than the first.

6. A multiple-baseline design might be considered when _____.
   a. the effects of a treatment cannot be reversed
   b. we want to test the effects of a treatment in multiple settings
   c. we do not want to use an *ABA* design for ethical reasons
   d. all of the above

7. To modify two or more behaviors, you might use a(n) _____ design.
   a. *ABAB*
   b. multiple-baseline
   c. discrete trials
   d. *ABCABC*

8. Which of the following is <u>not</u> true of small *N* designs?
   a. Statistics are not generally used to assess treatment effects.
   b. There are no statistics that can be used with small *N* designs.
   c. The use of statistics for small *N* designs is increasing.
   d. It is often possible to assess effects just by looking at the data.

9. All of the following small *N* designs except the _____ use baselines.
   a. *AB* design
   b. multiple-baseline design
   c. discrete trials design
   d. *ABABA* design

10. A small *N* design may have less _____ than a large *N* design.
    a. real-world significance
    b. internal validity
    c. external validity
    d. confounding

11. Which small N design would be most convincing?
    a. *AB*
    b. *ABACAD*
    c. *ABAB*
    d. *ABABA*

***Correct answers are located at the end of the chapter, but do not
look at them until you have completed the test.***

√ QUESTIONS FOR REVIEW AND STUDY

SHORT ESSAY: *use the information in the chapter to answer the following questions*

1. Explain how a small *N* design might detect effects that cannot be detected in a large *N* design.

2. What are some practical reasons for using a small *N* design?

3. How are treatment effects demonstrated in *ABA* designs?

4. Explain the uses of a multiple-baseline design.

5.   How does a discrete trials design differ from an *ABA* design?

6.   Discuss the major disadvantages of small N designs.

1.   Imagine that you read the following hypothetical headline in this week's *National Inquisitor.*

WOMAN CURED BY ALIEN FROM OUTER SPACE

Suppose the story went something like this:

> Dr. I. M. Delusional reported in last month's *Journal of Irreproducible Pseudoscience* that his former patient, Lotta H. Lucinations, was cured of long-standing paranoid delusions. Ms. Lucinations had been hospitalized because she believed she was being followed by agents of Interpol who wanted to gain possession of her unique ability to communicate with Venusians. While she was under hypnosis during a therapy session, the patient was observed by Dr. Delusional to be talking to someone or something that was not visible to him. Apparently, the invisible being, identified by Ms. Lucinations as a Venusian psychiatrist, cured the patient of her fears of Interpol by surrounding her with a cosmic aura of intergallactic invisibility--Interpol could no longer see her, so her fears abated, and she was released from the hospital. She has returned to her former job as the Assistant U.S. Secretary of Defense and has plans to star in her own late-night talk show on the SciFi Channel.
>
> Dr. Delusional is skeptical of claims that Ms. Lucinations was really cured by a Venusian psychiatrist. Instead, he maintains that he was responsible for curing the patient by planting a post-hypnotic suggestion that she would now be invisible to all agents of Interpol. In his article for the pseudoscientific journal, Dr. Delusional explains his hypnosis procedure and claims that his *AB* study provides incontrovertible proof that he--not a Venusian-- cured the patient. Ms. Lucinations, however, has refused to pay several thousand dollars in therapy bills from Dr. Delusional. A lawsuit is pending.

(Answer the questions on the next page about the news report you just read.)

(a) Given what you know about *AB* designs, do you think Dr. D. has proven his case? (Why not?)

(b) If Dr. D. believes that a reversal design would be unethical for his clinical patients, what other approaches could he consider to gain support for his position that a post-hypnotic suggestion can cure paranoid delusions?

(c) Explain how the Venusian psychiatrist (or something else) could be a potential history threat if Dr. D. decided to test his post-hypnotic suggestion hypothesis using an *ABA* design.

(d) Explain how a discrete trials design might be used to test whether post-hypnotic suggestions have effects or not.

√ RESEARCH IDEAS

1. The author's youngest dog, Samson, loves to play with both of the other Tibetan Mastiffs he lives with. When he is feeling playful, he will charge at them from across the room in an attempt to get them to play. Other times, he just wants to rub his face against theirs and lick them. Moose, the oldest, is very laid back, so he would just ignore Samson and go back to sleep. The middle TM, Lulu, has always been less tolerant. She would open her huge mouth and capture Samson's muzzle between her teeth. This was clearly painful for Samson, but he didn't change his behavior, so the author decided to use some behavior modification on Lulu.

   She selected a sophisticated verbal treatment recommended by many animal behaviorists: the "NO!--NO!--BAD DOG!" treatment. For a week beforehand, she tracked Lulu's behavior without any treatment. Then for a week she instituted the manipulation. Every time Lulu bit the younger dog, the author would scream "NO!--NO!--BAD DOG!" while keeping track of Lulu's behavior. Then for an additional week, she tracked Lulu's behavior without any manipulation. The results are graphed below.

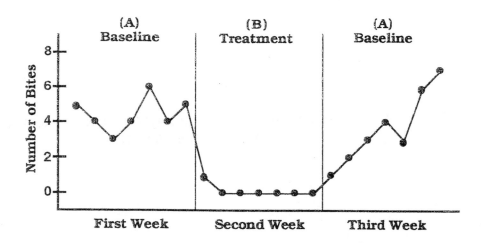

   (a) Did the treatment seem to work? How can you tell?

(The experiment continues on the next page.)

(b) Lulu is still biting Samson. What do you think the author should do now?

Even though the experiment seemed to work, the author realized afterward that there was a problem: Samson's behavior was not constant. Some days he approached Lulu several times; other days only once or twice. When the number of bites was converted to the percentage of time Lulu actually bit Samson, the results were somewhat different (see below).

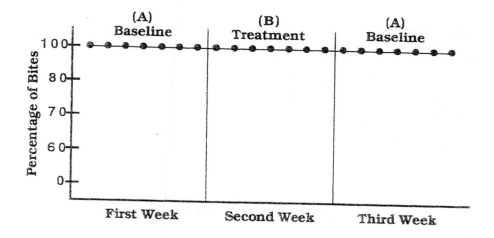

(c) Do you still think the treatment changed Lulu's behavior? If not, what do you think really happened?

(d) Clearly, Samson's inconsistent behavior confounded the experiment. What is this kind of confound called?

ANSWERS TO FILL-IN AND MULTIPLE CHOICE QUESTIONS

Fill-in

1. precision (298)
2. small *N* (300)
3. operant (300)
4. baseline (301)
5. *ABA* (303)
6. reinforcement; absenteeism (304)
7. three (305)
8. baseline (308)
9. multiple-baseline (309)
10. 50; 100 (311)
11. discrete trials (311)
12. subject (312)
13. 90 (313)
14. generalizability (315)
15. history (315)

Multiple choice

1. d (300)
2. b (303)
3. c (304)
4. d (308)
5. a (306)
6. d (309)
7. b (309)
8. b (311)
9. c (311)
10. c (312)
11. d (315)

SUGGESTED READINGS

Kazdin, A. E. (1992). *Research design in clinical psychology* (2nd edition). Boston: Allyn and Bacon.

Schweigert, W. A. (1994). *Research methods and statistics for psychology* (Chapter 11). Pacific Grove, CA: Brooks/Cole.

③PART THREE

RESULTS: COPING WITH DATA

The third major section of the textbook, called *Results*, parallels the Results section of a research report. The next three chapters explain statistical data analysis and present techniques for analyzing data from experiments using a number of different experimental designs. You will learn why we need statistics, how they work, and what is meant by statistical significance. You will also learn that statistical tests allow us to make probability statements about the results of experiments. They allow us to say that effects were (probably) produced by the independent variable(s), but statistically significant differences among the groups in an experiment do not prove that your research hypothesis is true. Instead, we obtain support for our experimental hypothesis (H_1) by ruling out the null hypothesis (H_0) that the scores sampled came from the same population. If the odds that the null hypothesis is true are very low (usually less than 5%, or $p < .05$), then, as long as the experiment was well-designed and well-conducted (and not confounded), we can be reasonably confident that our independent variable produced the observed differences between conditions.

By the time you have finished Part 3, you should be familiar with the most commonly used statistical tests. You should know (a) how to select the appropriate statistical tests, (b) how to compute several different kinds of statistics, (c) how to interpret the results of statistical tests, (d) how to put the results into words, and (e) how to describe your results in graphs and tables. In Chapters 12 through 14, you will learn how statistics provide an objective assessment of treatment effects.

Chapter 12: Why We Need Statistics
Chapter 13: Analyzing Results: Two Group Examples
Chapter 14: Analyzing Results: Multiple Groups and Factorial Experiments

12 CHAPTER TWELVE
Why We need Statistics

Chapter Outline

√√ CHAPTER OBJECTIVES: KEY CONCEPTS

Listed below are questions that test the major concepts you should know from Chapter 12. After reading the chapter, you should be able to answer each of the questions below. If not, go back to the book and read the appropriate sections again before continuing on in the Study Guide.

----

1.   What are <u>statistics</u> and why do we use them? (321)

2.   What is meant by the term <u>statistical inference</u>? (324)

3.   Explain <u>variability</u>. (324)

4.   What is the <u>null hypothesis</u>, and why do we attempt to reject it? (325)

5.   What is the <u>alternative hypothesis</u>, and why is it tested only indirectly in an experiment? (326)

6.   How are scores described in a <u>frequency distribution</u>? (328)

7.   What are the four steps in the <u>statistical inference</u> process? (329)

8.   Why must we consider the <u>variability</u> in our data when we attempt to reject H_0? (330)

9.   Describe the term <u>significance level</u>. What does $p<.05$ mean? (333)

10.   What are <u>Type 1 and Type 2 errors</u>? (336)

11.   How do <u>variability</u> and whether our hypothesis is <u>directional or nondirectional</u> influence the odds of finding significance? (339)

12.   Explain what is meant by critical regions. (340)

13.   What are <u>one-tailed and two-tailed tests</u>? (342)

14.   How do we <u>organize and summarize</u> experimental data? (345)

15.   Why is the <u>variance</u> used as a measure of variability, and how is it computed? (351)

√ QUESTIONS FOR REVIEW AND STUDY

KEY TERMS: *define each term using your own words*

Statistical inference (324):

Mean (324):

Variability (324):

Null hypothesis (H_0) (325):

Statistically significant (326):

Alternative hypothesis (H_1) (326):

Directional hypothesis (330):

Normal curve (331):

Significance level (333):

Experimental errors (335):

Type 1 error (336):

Type 2 error (336):

Critical regions (340):

Two-tailed test (342):

Nondirectional hypothesis (342):

One-tailed test (343):

Inferential statistics (344):

Test statistics (344):

Raw data (346):

Summary data (346):

Descriptive statistics (346):

Measures of central tendency (346):

Mode (346):

Median (346):

Variability (349):

Range (349):

Variance (351):

Standard deviation (353):

√ QUESTIONS FOR REVIEW AND STUDY

FILL INS: fill in the blanks with the right word or phrase

1. We use statistics because they allow us to evaluate our data _____.

2. We can never actually _____ that an independent variable had an effect.

3. Even though we test samples, statistics allow us to make inferences about the entire _____.

4. Instead of testing our research hypothesis directly, we formulate and test the _____ .

5. When our results are statistically significant, we can _____ the null hypothesis.

6. The more _____ there is in scores on the DV, the greater the difference between treatment groups has to be before we can reject the null hypothesis.

7. "Time passes quickly when you're having fun" is an example of a(n) _____ hypothesis.

8. A frequency distribution that is symmetrical and bell-shaped is called a(n) _____.

9. Because of variability, _____ will differ from one another.

10. A significance level of $p<.05$ means that we will reject H_0 if the pattern of data is so unlikely that it could have occurred by chance less than _____ % of the time.

11. Variations in subjects' scores produced by uncontrolled extraneous variables, such as experimenter bias, are called _____ errors.

12. The chance of mistakenly rejecting H_0 in an experiment is called _____ error.

13. When the IV has an effect, but we have failed to detect it, we have made a _____ error.

14. Large differences in treatment condition means are more likely in populations with _____ variability on the dependent measure.

15. With a directional hypothesis, we can use a _____ statistical test.

16. The statistics called the mode, median, and mean are known as measures of _____ .

17. The range, variance, and standard deviation are all measures of _____ .

Correct answers are located at the end of the chapter, but do not look at them until you have completed the test.

MULTIPLE CHOICE: circle the best answer to each question

---

1. Which of the following is <u>not</u> true of statistics?
    a. Many different kinds of statistics can be computed on a sample.
    b. Statistics allow us to evaluate data objectively.
    c. We prove that our treatment had an effect using statistics.
    d. Statistics allow us to make inferences about the larger population.

2. If we measure two or more groups on almost any dimension, we can expect _____ in their scores.
    a. variability
    b. unreliability
    c. stability
    d. similarity

3. Which of the following is <u>not</u> one of the steps in the process of statistical inference?
    a. sampling from a population
    b. stating a research hypothesis
    c. choosing a significance level
    d. evaluating the results using statistics

4. The hypothesis directly tested in an experiment is called the _____ hypothesis.
    a. experimental
    b. research
    c. alternative
    d. null

5. When the null hypothesis is true, _____ .
    a. there is very little variability in any of the treatment groups, making them appear to be from the same population
    b. it is still possible to make a Type 2 error but not a Type 1 error
    c. the independent variable did not have an effect because extraneous variables were not properly controlled
    d. scores of the treatment groups are so similar they appear to be from the same population

6. When different random samples from the same population are compared _____ .
   a. there will be differences in scores on the DV because of normal variability
   b. the variability will not usually differ, but scores on the DV will differ
   c. scores on the DV will differ when there is low variability
   d. scores will differ more than when convenience samples are compared

7. Which of the following is <u>not</u> necessarily true of frequency distributions of samples?
   a. The peak will represent the most frequently obtained score.
   b. They make it easy to examine an entire data set at the same time.
   c. Frequency is plotted on the horizontal or X axis of the graph.
   d. The curve will resemble the shape of a normal distribution.

8. In psychology experiments, statistics attaining significance levels less than _____ are considered statistically significant.
   a. .50
   b. .05
   c. .01
   d. .001

9. Significant differences between treatment groups are <u>more</u> likely when _____ .
   a. the IV has a large, rather than small, effect
   b. variability in scores on the DV is high
   c. the significance level is $p<.01$--not $p<.05$
   d. there is overlap in the treatment populations

10. _____ refers to the probability that the null hypothesis is true even when statistically significant results are obtained.
    a. Power
    b. Beta
    c. Type 1 error
    d. Type 2 error

11. Which of the following techniques would <u>not</u> reduce Type 2 error?
    a. Increase the number of subjects in each treatment group.
    b. Increase the effects of the independent variable.
    c. Decrease variability in scores on the DV.
    d. Decrease the alpha level from .05 to .01.

12. Making a Type 1 error is like _____ .
    a. putting a guilty person in jail
    b. putting an innocent person in jail
    c. letting a guilty person go free
    d. letting an innocent person go free

13. _____ differences between sample means are more likely in populations that have _____ variability.
    a. Small; high
    b. Large; high
    c. Significant; high
    d. Critical; normal

14. The hypothesis that cars driven on oil A will perform differently than cars driven on oil B requires a _____ .
    a. one-tailed test
    b. two-tailed test
    c. directional test
    d. largest-value test

15. The first step in analyzing data is _____ .
    a. selecting a statistical test
    b. summarizing it
    c. organizing it
    d. collecting it

16. Which of the following is not a measure of central tendency?
    a. mean
    b. median
    c. mode
    d. variance

17. The variance of a data set is _____ .
    a. the average squared deviation of scores from their mean
    b. the average deviation of scores about the mean
    c. the difference between the means of the largest and smallest scores
    d. the most common deviation of scores from their mean

Correct answers are located at the end of the chapter, but do not look at them until you have completed the test.

SHORT ESSAY: use the information in the chapter to answer the following questions

1. What are statistics? What do they do for us? What don't they do?

2. What is the null hypothesis in an experiment? What is the alternative hypothesis? What does it mean to reject the null hypothesis?

3.   What is a significance level, and why is it important?

4.   Explain how the odds of finding significance are influenced by variability in scores on the dependent measure.

5.   Discuss Type 1 and Type 2 errors and how each type may be minimized.

6.   What are the critical regions of a distribution of the differences between sample means? How are critical regions influenced by (1) variability, (2) significance levels, and (3) directional vs. nondirectional hypotheses?

√ EXERCISES AND APPLICATIONS

1. Here are more scores from Jay and John's warm/cold room experiment from Chapter 7 of the workbook. In part b you will create a frequency distribution of sample data that displays frequencies for the (1) warm room scores and the (2) cold room scores on the same graph.

Warm & Friendly (Jay)		Cold & Aloof (John)	
Warm room	Cold room	Warm room	Cold room
8	7	6	5
9	7	5	4
7	6	6	3
9	5	5	5
8	6	6	4
8	6	5	5
9	5	5	4
7	6	6	3
9	7	6	3
8	6	5	3

(a) First, list each different score obtained from subjects in the warm room. Then, count up the frequency with which any score appears. Counted data from the warm room are shown below, but you will need to count the data from the cold room.

Warm Room

Score	Count
5	5
6	5
7	2
8	4
9	4

Cold Room

Score	Count

(The exercise continues on the next page.)

(b) Use your counted data to create a frequency distribution below. Use a different color to plot your counts from the two different rooms. In cases in which no subject generated a certain score, count the frequency as zero. Connect the dots and label each curve you have created.

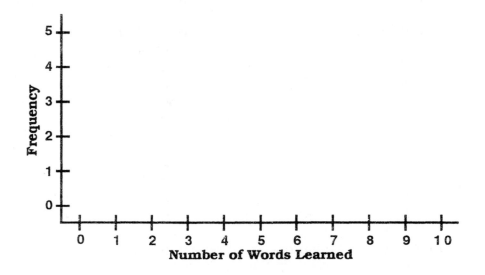

(c) Your curves should overlap. Without conducting statistical tests, can you really tell whether the temperature of the rooms produced significantly different scores just by looking at the frequency distribution?

(d) Do your sample scores appear to be normally distributed?

(The exercise continues on the next page.)

(e) Calculate the three measures of central tendency for each room condition:

               Warm Room   Cold Room

Mean:

Median:

Mode:

(f) Looking at your frequency distributions, which measure of central tendency gives the most accurate picture of the central tendency of each set of data? Why?

Warm Room:

Cold Room:

(g) Calculate the three measures of variability for each room condition. Show your calculations in the space below.

               Warm Room   Cold Room

Range:

Variance:

SD:

√ RESEARCH IDEAS

1.   Use descriptive statistics to summarize the data you collected in the simple between-subjects experiment on list learning from workbook Chapter 7. If you did not collect any data, you can generate hypothetical data sets by using the Random Number Table in Appendix B of your textbook.

(a) Write in data for 10 subjects below:

Time to Memorize List

List 1 (pronounceable)   List 2 (unpronounceable)

List 1 (pronounceable)	List 2 (unpronounceable)
1.	1.
2.	2.
3.	3.
4.	4.
5.	5.

(b) What was H_1 for this experiment? Is it directional or nondirectional?

(c) What was H_0 for this experiment?

(d) Calculate the three measures of central tendency for each condition.

List 1 (pronounceable)   List 2 (unpronounceable)

Mean:

Median:

Mode:

(The experiment continues on the next page.)

(e) Calculate the three measures of variability for each condition. Show
   your calculations below:

List 1 (pronounceable)   List 2 (unpronounceable)

Range:

Variance:

SD:

237

ANSWERS TO FILL-IN AND MULTIPLE CHOICE QUESTIONS

Fill-in

1. objectively (321)
2. prove (322)
3. population (324)
4. null hypothesis (325)
5. reject (326)
6. variability (330)
7. directional (330)
8. normal curve (331)
9. samples (331)
10. 5 (333)
11. experimental (335)
12. Type 1 (336)
13. Type 2 (336)
14. high (340)
15. one-tailed (343)
16. central tendency (346)
17. variability (349)

Multiple choice

1. c (321)
2. a (324)
3. b (325)
4. d (325)
5. d (325)
6. a (325)
7. c (328)
8. b (333)
9. a (335)
10. c (336)
11. d (336)
12. b (338)
13. b (340)
14. b (342)
15. c (345)
16. d (346)
17. a (351)

SUGGESTED READINGS

Kranzler, G., & Moursund, J. (1995). *Statistics for the terrified.* Englewood Cliffs, NJ: Prentice-Hall.

Salkind, N. J. (2000). *Statistics for people who (think they) hate statistics.* Thousand Oaks, CA: Sage Publications.

13 CHAPTER THIRTEEN
Analyzing Results: Two Group Examples

Chapter Outline

239

√√ CHAPTER OBJECTIVES: KEY CONCEPTS

Listed below are questions that test the major concepts you should know from Chapter 13. After reading the chapter, you should be able to answer each of the questions below. If not, go back to the book and read the appropriate sections again before continuing on in the Study Guide.

_____

1.   Why do we care about the kind of scale used to measure the dependent variable? What are the four levels of measurement? (361)

2.   What five questions do we need to ask to select a test for a two group experiment? (363)

3.   When do we use a chi square test? (364)

4.   How do we organize data for a chi square test? (365)

5.   What do the terms obtained and expected frequencies mean? (365)

6.   What are degrees of freedom? Why do we need to know about them? (366)

7. What is the critical value of X^2? (367)

8. When is a *t* test used? (368)

9. Why are sample size and degrees of freedom important for a *t* test? (369)

10. What does it mean to say that a statistical test, such as the *t* test, is robust? (370)

11. How do we decide whether to use a one- or two-tailed *t* test? (372)

12. What is the *t* test for independent groups, and when is it used? (372)

13. What is the *t* test for matched groups, and when is it used? (375)

√ QUESTIONS FOR REVIEW AND STUDY

KEY TERMS: *define each term using your own words*

Level of measurement (361):

Ratio scale (361):

Interval scale (361):

Ordinal scale (361):

Nominal scale (361):

Chi square (X^2) test (364):

Degrees of freedom (366):

Critical value (367):

t test (368):

Robust (370):

t test for independent groups (372):

t test for matched groups (378):

√ QUESTIONS FOR REVIEW AND STUDY

FILL INS: *fill in the blanks with the right word or phrase*

1.   The type of statistical test we use depends, in part, on the level of
      _____ used to measure the DV.

2.   The type of test to use also depends, in part, on the number of
      _____ variables in the experiment.

3.   An experiment with two treatment conditions and nominal data would
      use a(n) _____ test.

4.   The nonparametric X^2 test is one type of _____
      statistic.

5.   The X^2 test is less _____ than other, parametric
      tests.

6.   To conduct a X^2 test, we would need to calculate the expected
      _____ for the experimental data.

7.   To reject H_0, the computed value of X^2 must be at least as large as the
      tabled, _____ value.

8.   The critical values of test statistics are always organized by
      _____ rather than sample size.

9.   To analyze data from the time estimation experiment requires a *t* test for
      _____ groups.

10. With small samples, the *t* distribution has a _____ and _____ shape.

11. As the sample size and, thus, the degrees of freedom get smaller, the critical value of *t* needed to reject H$_0$ gets _____.

12. If our hypothesis is directional, we could use a _____ -tailed test.

13. If the computed value of *t* is less extreme than the critical value, the most likely cause of group differences is _____.

14. For a two group, between-subjects experiment with ratio data, we would select a *t* test for _____ groups.

15. The numerator of the formula for a *t* test for independent groups is the difference between the _____ of the groups.

16. The denominator of the formula for a *t* test for independent groups is an estimate of _____ .

17. The numerator of the formula for a within-subjects *t* test is the difference between _____ of scores.

18. We end up with fewer _____ in a within-subjects *t* than in a *t* test for independent groups.

19. When we use a matched groups or a within-subjects design, we _____ the amount of variability produced by factors other than the independent variable.

Correct answers are located at the end of the chapter, but do not look at them until you have completed the test.

√ QUESTIONS FOR REVIEW AND STUDY

MULTIPLE CHOICE: circle the best answer to each question

1. Which of the following is <u>not</u> related to our choice of a statistical test?
   a. the number of independent variables
   b. the level of measurement used for the DV
   c. whether the design is within- or between-subjects
   d. the number of subjects in each treatment condition

2. In the priming experiment described in the textbook, subjects in the priming condition made more frequent errors on the test question than subjects in the control group. This experiment would be analyzed using a _____ .
   a. *t* test for independent groups
   b. *t* test for matched groups
   c. Mann-Whitney *U* test
   d. X^2 test

3. The null hypothesis for a chi square test is _____ .
   a. $O = E$
   b. $O \div E = 0$
   c. $H_0 = H_1$
   d. $H_O = H_E$

4. We would select the appropriate distribution for chi square based on _____.
   a. the total number of subjects
   b. the degrees of freedom
   c. whether the null hypothesis was rejected or not
   d. the numerator of the formula

5. One advantage of computer statistical analysis programs is that _____.
   a. they will automatically interpret the results for you
   b. they are more accurate than hand-calculated statistics
   c. the probability value of the obtained statistical value is given
   d. they will select the appropriate test for your data

6. Which of the following is not true for small samples?
   a. Their means usually vary more from the population mean than do means of large samples.
   b. Their population means will be less normally distributed than the population means of large samples.
   c. It is more difficult to reject the null hypothesis than it is with large samples.
   d. The critical values of test statistics are larger for small samples than for large samples.

7. With 15 or 20 subjects in each group, assumptions of the t test may be violated because the test is _____ .
   a. normally distributed
   b. inferential
   c. robust
   d. individual

8. Which of the following questions does not need to be answered in order to use the statistical table for t?
   a. Is the hypothesis directional or nondirectional?
   b. How many degrees of freedom do we have?
   c. What significance level are we using?
   d. How many treatment conditions do we have?

9. To reject the null hypothesis, the obtained value of a statistic must _____ the critical value.
   a. be equal to
   b. exceed
   c. be equal to or exceed
   d. be less extreme than

10. A two group, between-subjects experiment testing the effects of room temperatures (cold vs. warm) on the time it takes to learn a list of words would be analyzed using a _____.
    a. t test for independent groups
    b. t test for matched groups
    c. chi square test
    d. X^2 test

11. To test the prediction that it would take less time to learn a word list in a warm room than in a cold room (#10), we could use a _____.
    a. one-tailed t test
    b. two-tailed t test
    c. nondirectional x^2 test
    d. directional x^2 test

12. Which of the following makes up the denominator of the formula for the t test for independent groups?
    a. differences between pairs of scores
    b. differences between the means of the two treatment groups
    c. variances and the number of subjects in each group
    d. the degrees of freedom for each treatment condition

13. A t test for matched groups is also called a(n) _____ .
    a. independent-groups t test
    b. directional t test
    c. random-groups t test
    d. within-subjects t test

14. The t test for matched groups uses _____ .
    a. a family of t distributions with smaller critical regions
    b. the same family of t distributions as the t test for independent groups
    c. t distributions with one less df than the t test for independent groups
    d. N - 1 t distributions

15. The numerator in the formula for the t test for matched groups represents _____ .
    a. differences between means of the two groups
    b. differences between pairs of scores
    c. degrees of freedom
    d. the number of subjects

16. The t test for matched groups is usually more powerful, even though it has a smaller number of _____ .
    a. degrees of freedom
    b. critical values
    c. calculations
    d. responses

Correct answers are located at the end of the chapter, but do not look at them until you have completed the test.

√ QUESTIONS FOR REVIEW AND STUDY

SHORT ESSAY: use the information in the chapter to answer the following questions

1. What five questions need to be answered in order to select a statistical test?

2. What is a chi square (x^2) test, and when is it used? After the x^2 is calculated, how do you know whether it is significant or not?

3.   What are degrees of freedom, and why do we need to know about them? How do they (along with sample size) influence statistical significance?

4.   What is the *t* test for independent groups, and when is it used? What does the *t* formula represent?

5. What is a *t* test for matched groups, and when is it used? Conceptually, how is the formula different from the formula for the *t* test for independent groups?

6. Compare the power of the two types of *t* tests to detect a significant effect.

1. Consider the following hypothetical survey results: In a cable television poll, 32 young men and women who liked to watch music videos on TV were asked whether they preferred the music on MTV (M) or on VH1 (V). Their data are shown below:

Men		Women	
S_1 = M	S_2 = V	S_1 = V	S_2 = M
S_3 = M	S_4 = M	S_3 = V	S_4 = V
S_5 = V	S_6 = M	S_5 = M	S_6 = M
S_7 = M	S_8 = M	S_7 = M	S_8 = V
S_9 = M	S_{10} = M	S_9 = V	S_{10} = V
S_{11} = M	S_{12} = M	S_{11} = V	S_{12} = V
S_{13} = M	S_{14} = V	S_{13} = V	S_{14} = V
S_{15} = V	S_{16} = M	S_{15} = V	S_{16} = M

(a) First, create a 2 X 2 contingency table. Tabulate the obtained frequencies that belong in the table below:

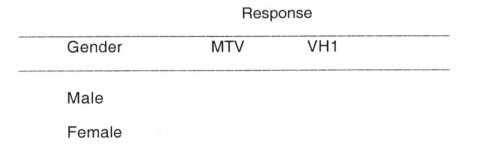

Response

Gender	MTV	VH1
Male		
Female		

(b) Next, compute the row and column totals and calculate the expected frequencies for each of the four cells.

(c) Compute the chi square. Show your work below.

(The exercise continues on the next page.)
(d) Using $p<.05$ as the significance level, look up the critical value of X^2 in Appendix B2 of the text. Can you reject the null hypothesis that there is no difference in preferences between men and women?

(e) Using the table in Appendix B2, what is the smallest probability level at which your obtained value remains significant?

(f) Compare your results with those obtained by StatView.

Contingency Table Analysis

Summary Statistics

DF:	1	
Total Chi-Square:	6.149	p = .0131
G Statistic:	6.367	
Contingency Coefficient:	.401	
Phi:	.438	
Chi-Square with continuity correction:	4.518	p = .0335

(g) Now, interpret your results using the three-step process illustrated in Chapter 13 (p. 367).

1.

2.

3.

√ RESEARCH IDEAS

1. Let's return to the music video experiment from Research Ideas at the end of workbook Chapter 8. Below are the scores of the 32 matched young men. (>1 hour per week = frequently watch [F]; <1 hour per week = seldom watch [S].)

Sexual Videos				Nonsexual Videos			
$F_1 =$ 8	$F_2 =$ 7			$F_1 =$ 5	$F_2 =$ 6		
$F_3 =$ 7	$F_4 =$ 6			$F_3 =$ 4	$F_4 =$ 5		
$F_5 =$ 4	$F_6 =$ 6			$F_5 =$ 5	$F_6 =$ 7		
$F_7 =$ 5	$F_8 =$ 8			$F_7 =$ 4	$F_8 =$ 5		
$S_1 =$ 2	$S_2 =$ 2			$S_1 =$ 6	$S_2 =$ 3		
$S_3 =$ 3	$S_4 =$ 3			$S_3 =$ 5	$S_4 =$ 6		
$S_5 =$ 1	$S_6 =$ 4			$S_5 =$ 4	$S_6 =$ 4		
$S_7 =$ 3	$S_8 =$ 3			$S_7 =$ 4	$S_8 =$ 7		

You already calculated the mean (average) mood score for the two video conditions. The means were:

Sexual Videos Group = 4.5
Nonsexual Videos Group = 5.0

Looking at the means, it appeared that, overall, subjects felt happier after the nonsexual videos than after the sexual videos, but were they significantly happier? To find out, you will need to conduct a statistical test.

(a) There was one independent variable, two treatment conditions with matched subjects, and interval scale data. Which *t* test will you use?

(b) What are the degrees of freedom for this experiment (N - 1 pairs of scores)?

(c) From Appendix B3 in the text, what critical value of *t* is needed to reject the null hypothesis?

(The second part of the experiment continues on the next page.)

254

(d) Calculate your *t* value. Assume your hypothesis was nondirectional and your significance level was $p<.05$. If you have access to a computer statistics package, you may use it. Tape the summary table in the space below. Otherwise, calculate the *t* value by hand, showing your work below:

(e) Clearly, from the results obtained from the statistical test, you are unable to reject the null hypothesis for this experiment. Interpret the results in the form illustrated in textbook Chapter 13 (p. 375).

1.

2.

3.

(f) Calculate the effect size *r*.

ANSWERS TO FILL-IN AND MULTIPLE CHOICE QUESTIONS

Fill-in

1. measurement (361)
2. independent (363)
3. chi square (362)
4. inferential (363)
5. powerful (364)
6. frequencies (364)
7. critical (366)
8. degrees of freedom (367)
9. independent (368)
10. flatter; wider (369)
11. larger (371)
12. one (372)
13. chance (372)
14. independent (372)
15. means (373)
16. variability (373)
17. pairs (381)
18. degrees of freedom (381)
19. lower (381)

Multiple choice

1. d (360)
2. d (363)
3. a (365)
4. b (366)
5. c (367)
6. a (370)
7. c (370)
8. d (372)
9. b (372)
10. a (372)
11. a (372)
12. c (373)
13. d (378)
14. b (378)
15. b (381)
16. a (381)

SUGGESTED READINGS

Kranzler, G., & Moursund, J. (1995). *Statistics for the terrified.* Englewood Cliffs, NJ: Prentice-Hall.

Salkind, N. J. (2000). *Statistics for people who (think they) hate statistics.* Thousand Oaks, CA: Sage Publications.

14 CHAPTER FOURTEEN
Analyzing Results: Multiple Groups and Factorial Experiments

Chapter Outline

257

√√ CHAPTER OBJECTIVES: KEY CONCEPTS

Listed below are questions that test the major concepts you should know from Chapter 14. After reading the chapter, you should be able to answer each of the questions below. If not, go back to the book and read the appropriate sections again before continuing on in the Study Guide.

----

1.   When do we use <u>analysis of variance</u>? (388)

2.   What are the sources of variability that comprise <u>error</u>? (390)

3.   What contributes to <u>within-groups variability</u> in an experiment with one independent variable? (391)

4.   What contributes to <u>between-groups variability</u>? (391)

5.   What are the components of an <u>*F* ratio</u>? (391)

6.   Explain a <u>one-way between-subjects ANOVA</u>. When is it used? (392)

7. What is the logic behind calculating the MS_W and MS_B? Where does each go in the ANOVA formula? (395-398)

8. Once you have calculated an F value, how do you find the appropriate critical value? (399)

9. What is the influence of degrees of freedom (and sample size) on the critical value? (399)

10. When are post hoc tests needed? What are a priori comparisons? (401-402)

11. When is a one-way repeated measures ANOVA needed? (405)

12. What is a two-way ANOVA, and when is it used? Conceptually, how is it different from a one-way ANOVA? (406-407)

13. Give an example of an experiment that requires (a) an ANOVA for mixed designs and (b) a repeated measures ANOVA. (419)

√ QUESTIONS FOR REVIEW AND STUDY

KEY TERMS: *define each term using your own words*

Analysis of variance (388):

Within-groups variability (389):

Between-groups variability (389):

Error (390):

F ratio (391):

One-way between-subjects ANOVA (392):

Sum of squares (394):

SS_W (394):

MS (394):

MS_W (395):

Grand mean (396):

SS_B (396):

MS_B (396):

Post hoc tests (401):

A priori comparisons (402):

One-way repeated measures ANOVA (405):

Main effect (405):

Two-way ANOVA (408):

Interaction (413):

√ QUESTIONS FOR REVIEW AND STUDY

FILL INS: *fill in the blanks with the right word or phrase*

1. Multiple groups and factorial designs with interval or ratio data are analyzed using _____.

2. The extent to which subjects' scores differ from one another under the same treatment conditions is called _____ variability.

3. _____ variability is the extent to which group performance differs from one treatment condition to another.

4. Unwanted variability produced by individual differences, mistakes in recording data, variations in testing conditions, and so forth, is called _____.

5. The larger the effect of the independent variable, the larger the value of the _____ should be.

6. As with *t*, *F* is actually a whole family of _____.

7. In a multiple groups experiment using interval or ratio data, we would analyze the results using a(n) _____ between-subjects ANOVA.

8. The sum of squared deviations from the group mean is called the _____ .

9. The average squared deviation from the mean is called the

_____.

10. F equals MS___ divided by MS___ .

11. The critical value needed to reject H_0 becomes less extreme as sample size and, thus, _____ increase.

12. ANOVA computations are summarized and presented in a(n) _____ table.

13. When results are graphed, the vertical axis should be about _____ the size of the horizontal axis.

14. When a significant F value is obtained for a one-way ANOVA, the group differences must be pinpointed using _____ tests or _____ comparisons.

15. Sometimes, experimenters use statistics (e.g., ANCOVA) to control for the effects of _____ variables, such as subject variables.

16. A 2 X 2 factorial experiment would be analyzed using a(n) _____ analysis of variance.

17. ANOVAs for factorials are more complex because effects of the _____ (s) must also be computed.

Correct answers are located at the end of the chapter, but do not look at them until you have completed the test.

√ QUESTIONS FOR REVIEW AND STUDY

MULTIPLE CHOICE: *circle the best answer to each question*

---

1. When subjects are randomly assigned to conditions, which of the following should contribute to between-groups, but not within-groups, variability?
   a. experimental error
   b. treatment effects
   c. individual differences
   d. mistakes in recording data

2. An *F* ratio can be represented by all of the following except _____ .
   a. variability from treatment effects and error ÷ variability from error
   b. variability between groups ÷ variability within groups
   c. *df* between groups ÷ *df* within groups
   d. mean square between groups ÷ mean square within groups

3. To analyze a three independent groups experiment using interval data, we would use a _____ analysis of variance.
   a. one-way between-subjects
   b. repeated measures
   c. two-way between-subjects
   d. mixed factorial

4. Which of the following is <u>not</u> an assumption of between-subjects analysis of variance procedures?
   a. homogeneity of population variances
   b. the populations are normally distributed
   c. the groups are independent
   d. the treatment effect is robust

5. Which of the following is <u>not</u> computed in a one-way between-subjects analysis of variance?
   a. $MS_{1 X 2}$
   b. SS_B
   c. MS_B
   d. MS_W

6. In a one-way between-subjects ANOVA, treatment effects are represented in _____ .
    a. MS_W
    b. MS_B
    c. *df*
    d. S S

7. Which of the following is <u>not</u> needed to test the significance of an *F* value?
    a. the critical value
    b. df_W
    c. df_B
    d. sample size

8. When graphing data, values of _____ are plotted on the vertical axis.
    a. the dependent variable
    b. the independent variable
    c. factor 1
    d. factor 2

9. In which of the following cases would post hoc tests be necessary?
    a. a significant F for a two-group experiment
    b. a significant F for a three-group experiment
    c. a significant main effect in a 2 X 2 factorial
    d. all of the above

10. We do not generally worry about increasing our odds of a Type 1 error when doing a priori comparisons as long as _____.
    a. we are not using a set of *t* tests
    b. the effects are statistically significant
    c. the number of tests is less than the number of treatment groups
    d. $N - p$ or fewer planned comparisons are conducted

11. Which of the following is not accomplished by using an ANCOVA?
    a. control over moderating variables
    b. a refined estimate of experimental error
    c. adjustment for preexisting group differences
    d. transforming distributions to approximate normality

12. Which of the following tests would be used to analyze an experiment in which subjects received all three of the treatment conditions?
   a. one-way between-subjects ANOVA
   b. within-subjects t tests
   c. one-way repeated measures ANOVA
   d. two-way repeated measures ANOVA

13. In a two-way ANOVA, between-groups variability includes all of the following except _____ .
   a. variability associated with factor 1
   b. variability associated with factor 2
   c. variability associated with the interaction between the factors
   d. variability associated with the higher-order interactions

14. When we compute SS_1 for a two-way ANOVA, we _____ the data across the other experimental conditions.
   a. eliminate
   b. collapse
   c. control
   d. evaluate

15. Suppose the computed F value for a two-way interaction was 0.00. This implies that _____.
   a. the two factors did not interact
   b. there was no treatment effect
   c. within-groups variability exceeded between-groups variability
   d. between-group variability exceeded within-groups variability

16. An experiment with one within-subjects factor and two between-subjects factors would be analyzed with a _____ ANOVA.
   a. repeated measures
   b. one-way
   c. mixed factorial
   d. two-way

Correct answers are located at the end of the chapter, but do not look at them until you have completed the test.

√ QUESTIONS FOR REVIEW AND STUDY

SHORT ESSAY: use the information in the chapter to answer the following questions

1.   What kinds of experiments require an analysis of variance?

2.   What are the sources of variability in an experiment that contribute to error?

3.   What are the sources in an experiment that contribute to between-groups (but not within-groups) variability?

4.   Describe three ways of conceptualizing the F ratio in a one-way ANOVA.

5. How is variability broken down in a two-way ANOVA?

6. What ANOVA procedures are available for (a) within-subjects experiments with one independent variable, (b) within-subjects factorial experiments, and (c) experiments that contain both between-subjects and within-subjects factors?

√ EXERCISES AND APPLICATIONS

1. Erik conducted a between-subjects experiment testing six different values of the independent variable, light levels, on the time it takes to learn a list of 10 word-pairs. He decided that the formula for a t test was much simpler than the formula for a one-way analysis of variance, so he analyzed his data using multiple t tests, comparing two groups at a time. The formula for determining all possible pairs of groups in an experiment is shown below. (N represents the number of groups in the experiment.)

$$\frac{N(N-1)}{2}$$

   (a) How many t tests would he have to conduct in all?

   (b) Assuming that Type 1 error is cumulative, what would his total probability of Type 1 error be if he uses a $p<.05$ significance level?

   (c) If Erik found that the statistical analysis was significant, would you be convinced? If not, why?

   (d) If he obtained significance at $p < .05$ using a one-way ANOVA, what would be the probability of Type 1 error?

   (e) If the ANOVA was significant, what could Erik say about his treatment without further tests?

   (f) What tests would he need to conduct?

(The exercise continues on the next page.)

(g) Here are the hypothetical data (rounded to the nearest minute) from Erik's experiment:

Light Levels

	1	2	3	4	5	6
S_1	7	6	6	7	3	4
S_2	6	6	5	5	3	3
S_3	7	6	6	7	3	4
S_4	7	7	6	6	4	3
S_5	6	6	5	5	3	3

Compute a one-way analysis of variance on Erik's data, and fill in the blanks in the summary table below:

Source	df	SS	MS	F
Between groups	5			
Within groups	24			
Total	29			

(h) Clearly, the analysis of variance was statistically significant! Before you can interpret the effects, however, you still need follow-up tests. Post hoc tests conducted on the group means produced the results below. (Means sharing the same subscript do not differ from each other.)

Light Level Groups

1	2	3	4	5	6
6.6_a	6.2_a	5.6_a	6.0_a	3.2_b	3.4_b

Using the obtained results, interpret the effects of light levels on the time it took to learn the word-pair list in the manner illustrated on p. 403 of the text:

1.

2.

3.

√ RESEARCH IDEAS

1. Once again, here are the scores from Jay and John's warm/cold room experiment from Chapter 12. The appropriate analysis to conduct on these data would be a two-way between-subjects ANOVA. This would allow us to investigate (a) the effects of the two room temperatures, (b) the effects of the two experimenters, and (c) the interaction between the two.

Warm & Friendly (Jay)		Cold & Aloof (John)	
Warm room	Cold room	Warm room	Cold room
8	7	6	5
9	7	5	4
7	6	6	3
9	5	5	5
8	6	6	4
8	6	5	5
9	5	5	4
7	6	6	3
9	7	6	3
8	6	5	3

(a) Conduct a two-way ANOVA. If you have access to a computer statistics program, you may use it; otherwise calculate the *F* ratios by hand, and fill in the summary table below:

Source	df	SS	MS	F	p value
Between groups					
Experimenter	1				
Room	1				
Interaction	1				
Within groups	36				
Total	39				

(Continues on the next page.)

(b) Write out the design in shorthand notation and label the variables:

(c) Diagram the experiment in a design matrix, and put the group means inside the cells:

(d) In this experiment there were two significant main effects, but the interaction was not significant. Post hoc tests are not required. Why not?

(e) Interpret the significant main effect for the experimenter factor (Jay vs. John):

(f) Interpret the significant main effect for the room factor (Warm vs. Cold):

(g) Calculate effect sizes for the two significant effects:

ANSWERS TO FILL-IN AND MULTIPLE CHOICE QUESTIONS

Fill-in

1. analysis of variance (388)
2. within-groups (389)
3. Between-groups (389)
4. error (390)
5. *F* ratio (391)
6. distributions (391)
7. one-way (392)
8. sum of squares (394)
9. mean square (394)
10. B; W (398)
11. degress of freedom (399)
12. summary (399)
13. 3/4 (400)
14. post hoc; a priori (401, 402)
15. moderating (404)
16. two-way (406)
17. interaction (407)

Multiple choice

1. b (391)
2. c (391, 398)
3. a (392)
4. d (393)
5. a (395)
6. b (396)
7. d (398)
8. a (400)
9. b (401)
10. c (402)
11. d (404)
12. c (405)
13. d (407)
14. b (412)
15. a (416)
16. c (419)

SUGGESTED READINGS

Gonick, L., & Smith, W. (1993). *The cartoon guide to statistics.* New York: HarperCollins.

Kranzler, G., & Moursund, J. (1995). *Statistics for the terrified.* Englewood Cliffs, NJ: Prentice-Hall.

Salkind, N. J. (2000). *Statistics for people who (think they) hate statistics.* Thousand Oaks, CA: Sage Publications.

4 PART FOUR

DISCUSSION

The final section of the textbook, called *Discussion,* parallels the Discussion section of the research report. These two chapters will explain how we evaluate an experiment (from the inside and from the outside) and how we incorporate this evaluation into the Discussion section of a report.

By now, you already know that the most important kind of validity for an experiment is internal validity. Without internal validity, external validity is a moot point. It would not make sense to attempt to generalize the findings from an internally invalid experiment! Only experiments that are internally valid can be used to make cause and effect statements about behavior--the goal of experimentation. Chapter 15 explains the steps researchers take to evaluate the internal and external validity of their own experiments. Researchers evaluate their own experiments and report any flaws or shortcomings honestly in the Discussion. A reviewer may reject your report entirely if you have missed major flaws in your experiment. Researchers also discuss their results in light of past research, explain inconsistencies between their findings and those of others, and point out plausible alternative explanations for their findings. Any limitations on generalizability are also discussed.

By the time you have finished Part 4, you should be able to write up your findings in a research report in the accepted style of the American Psychological Association. An actual published article is annotated in depth so that you can see exactly what kind of information goes in each major section of the report. We have found that the best way to learn to write good reports is to work from a model, so we have provided one for you. When you type your report, however, your typed manuscript will not look like the published version. Instead, you will need to follow APA's word-processing guidelines (discussed in textbook Chapter 16). A model for you to use when typing your report is provided in Appendix C.

Chapter 15: Drawing Conclusions: The Search for the Elusive Bottom Line
Chapter 16: Writing the Research Report

15 CHAPTER FIFTEEN
Drawing Conclusions: The Search for the Elusive Bottom Line

Chapter Outline

√√ CHAPTER OBJECTIVES: KEY CONCEPTS

Listed below are questions that test the major concepts you should know from Chapter 15. After reading the chapter, you should be able to answer each of the questions below. If not, go back to the book and read the appropriate sections again before continuing on in the Study Guide.

_____

1. What does it mean to say that our results are <u>statistically significant</u>? (429)

2. What are some ways to evaluate <u>internal validity</u> after an experiment has been conducted? (432)

3. How can Orne's (1969) "<u>pact of ignorance</u>" affect our ability to evaluate internal validity? (433)

4. What does the term <u>statistical conclusion validity</u> mean? (434)

5. What are the two basic requirements for <u>external validity</u>? (435)

6.   How do we determine the <u>generalizability</u> of results <u>across subjects</u>? (436)

7.   Can you explain why researchers need to use qualifying statements when they attempt to <u>generalize from their procedures to more general concepts</u>? (437)

8.   What are the four types of <u>aggregation</u> discussed in the text? (440)

9.   What are <u>multivariate designs</u>, and how can they increase external validity? (441)

10.   Why are <u>nonreactive measures</u> more generalizable? (442)

11.   What are the benefits of <u>field experiments</u>? (444)

12.   If you <u>did not obtain significant results</u>, what approaches can you use to evaluate the experiment? (445)

√ QUESTIONS FOR REVIEW AND STUDY

KEY TERMS: *define each term using your own words*

Manipulation check (432):

Statistical-conclusion validity (434):

Effect size (435):

Aggregation (440):

Multivariate design (441):

Multivariate analysis of variance (442):

Reactivity (442):

Unobtrusive measures (443):

Field experiment (444):

√ QUESTIONS FOR REVIEW AND STUDY

FILL INS: *fill in the blanks with the right word or phrase*

1. Statistical significance tells us nothing about the _____ of the experiment.

2. When we evaluate an experiment, we begin by judging the _____ validity.

3. Knowing whether subjects guessed the hypothesis is often difficult because a _____ might form between subjects and experimenters.

4. When a test statistic is used inappropriately, an experiment will lack _____ validity.

5. The _____ is an estimate of the magnitude of the treatment effect(s).

6. If the results of an experiment can be accurately extended to other situations, the experiment has _____ validity.

7. Generality across subjects can sometimes be explored within the same experiment by including a _____ variable as an independent variable.

8. When the findings of different experiments seem to conflict, it may be that different _____ definitions were used.

9.   When data gathered in various ways are grouped together and averaged, it is called _____.

10. The use of multiple ways of measuring the dependent variable in an experiment is known as aggregation over _____.

11. It is possible to investigate many dependent variables in the same experiment using a _____ design.

12. An experiment with multiple IVs and DVs that uses ratio or interval data can be analyzed using a _____.

13. The use of _____ measures is a good way to minimize reactivity in an experiment.

14. We can increase the external validity of a laboratory finding by conducting a _____ experiment.

15. Miller (1977) has argued for the use of _____ _____ to validate the results of laboratory experiments.

16. The presence of confounding or numerous uncontrolled variables in an experiment suggest faulty _____.

17. Researchers need to consider the possibility that nonsignificant results in a well-designed and well-conducted experiment could have been caused by a faulty _____.

Correct answers are located at the end of the chapter, but do not look at them until you have completed the test.

√ QUESTIONS FOR REVIEW AND STUDY

MULTIPLE CHOICE: circle the best answer to each question

1. A measure of the success of the experimental procedures to create the conditions you intended is called a(n) _____ .
   a. manipulation check
   b. nonreactive measure
   c. unobtrusive measure
   d. informal interview

2. Which of the following is <u>not</u> related to statistical-conclusion validity?
   a. the number of statistical tests conducted
   b. the meaningfulness of the effect obtained
   c. the kind of statistical tests employed
   d. the assumptions behind the statistical tests used

3. When an experiment has external validity, we can generalize the results using _____ .
   a. deduction
   b. induction
   c. obduction
   d. reduction

4. Results that are externally valid meet two basic requirements: they are internally valid, and they can be _____ .
   a. demonstrated
   b. tested
   c. manipulated
   d. replicated

5. To extend the external validity of an experiment to people of different ages, an experimenter might use different age groups as a(n) _____ .
   a. independent variable
   b. dependent variable
   c. covariate
   d. multivariate

6. Researchers qualify the conclusions they draw from significant results because _____ .
   a. there is always a possibility of Type 2 error
   b. scientists are basically conservative in their opinions
   c. the nature of experimentation is probabilistic
   d. their findings may contradict findings from other researchers

7. Which of the following is not one of the procedures for increasing external validity?
   a. multivariate designs
   b. aggregation
   c. field experiments
   d. manipulation checks

8. Which of the following is not one of the types of aggregation?
   a. aggregation over subjects
   b. aggregation over situations
   c. aggregation over trials
   d. aggregation over effects

9. Which of the following is recommended for aggregation over measures?
   a. adding subjects to the experiment
   b. the use of multivariate designs
   c. using an ANCOVA
   d. increasing the range of experimental stimuli

10. Taking multiple measures of the dependent variable will result in all of the following except _____ .
   a. it will reduce the chance of Type 1 error
   b. it will offset errors from a single, inadequate measure
   c. it increases our confidence in the results
   d. it increases external validity

11. Using unobtrusive measures will _____ .
   a. avoid practical problems
   b. increase internal validity
   c. minimize reactivity
   d. reduce confounding

12. Which of the following is <u>not</u> a benefit of field experiments?
    a. They can be used to make cause and effect statements.
    b. They produce more realistic effects
    c. They increase external validity
    d. They decrease Type 1 and 2 errors.

13. A researcher who gets nonsignificant results should do all of the following except _____.
    a. evaluate the hypothesis
    b. evaluate the procedures
    c. consider the possibility of a Type 1 error
    d. consider the possibility of a Type 2 error

14. Low power in an experiment can be produced by all of the following except _____.
    a. not enough subjects
    b. small error variance
    c. a weak manipulation
    d. inconsistent procedures

15. Sometimes, nonsignificant results are produced because all subjects use only the bottom end of a scale. This problem is called a _____ effect.
    a. ceiling
    b. Ben & Jerry
    c. needle in a haystack
    d. floor

16. When would a researcher who obtained nonsignificant results need to reconsider the experimental hypothesis?
    a. when the experiment was executed properly
    b. when attempting to publish the results
    c. when the results are almost significant, say $p < .10$.
    d. when the experiment contained numerous uncontrolled variables

Correct answers are located at the end of the chapter, but do not look at them until you have completed the test.

√ QUESTIONS FOR REVIEW AND STUDY

SHORT ESSAY: *use the information in the chapter to answer the following questions*

1. Your experiment produced a significant effect. What conclusions can you draw?

2. What should a researcher consider in evaluating an experiment's internal validity?

3.   What problems can occur in evaluating internal validity if a "pact of ignorance" forms between subjects and experimenters?

4.   What factors can reduce statistical conclusion validity?

5.   Discuss each of the four different types of aggregation discussed in the text.

6.   What does a researcher need to consider when the results of an experiment are not significant?

√ EXERCISES AND APPLICATIONS

1.   Imagine that a novice researcher conducted the following experiment to investigate the effects of film violence on children:

One hundred 9-year-olds (50 boys and 50 girls) from a local elementary school were randomly assigned to two different treatment groups. Kids in the low-violence group watched "The Muppet Movie" in the school library, while the high-violence group watched "Rambo, Part X " in the school gym.

After the movies ended, all the children were allowed to go out to the playground for a half-hour recess. So that the researcher could identify the subjects in each treatment group, kids who saw "The Muppet Movie" were given white hats to wear; kids who saw "Rambo" were given black hats.

The dependent variable, aggressiveness, was defined as the number of arguments children were involved in during the recess. The researcher and several assistants hid in the bushes where they could observe the kids and record arguments. The mean number of arguments* in each condition is shown below:

| | Subjects | | |
Film	Girls	Boys	Condition Means
Low Violence	4.0a	6.0a	5.0
High Violence	5.0a	9.0b	7.0
Condition Means	4.5	7.5	

A 2 (Subjects) X 2 (Film) ANOVA produced the following effects:

1. Main effect for Subjects: $F(1,96) = 6.88$, $p<.05$
2. Main effect for Film: $F(1,96) = 13.56$, $p<.01$
3. Interaction: $F(1,96) = 9.31$, $p<.01$

* Results of post hoc tests on the significant interaction are represented by subscripts (means sharing the same subscript do not differ, $p<.05$).

(The exercise continues on the next page.)

(a) Using the statistics presented, interpret the two significant main effects:

1.

2.

(b) Graph the significant interaction below using a line graph. Be sure to label the lines correctly.

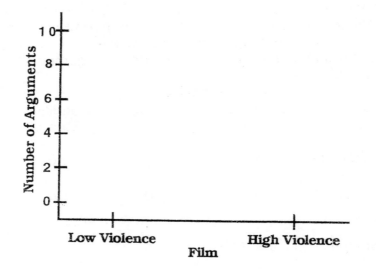

(c) Interpret the interaction:

(The exercise continues on the next page.)

(d) Calculate effect sizes for each of the significant effects. Which effect (Subjects, Film, or the interaction between both factors) was largest?

(e) Now, using what you have learned in Chapter 15, evaluate the experiment from the inside (internal validity). The experiment has a number of serious flaws that reduce internal validity. One, the color of the hats, is given as an example. Name three others and explain why they reduce the experiment's internal validity:

1. *Color of the hats: There is a common stereotype that good guys wear white and bad guys wear black. It is possible that the children's behavior and/or the researchers' recordings were influenced by this rather than by the type of film.*

2.

3.

4.

(The exercise continues on the next page.)

(f) For each potential confound identified, design a more valid procedure:

1. *Hats:*

2.

3.

4.

(g) Evaluate the experiment's external validity. (Hint: Are the two basic requirements met?)

(h) Next, pretend for the moment that the experiment was internally valid and could be replicated. Now, evaluate the external validity (across subjects, across procedures, and across situations):

Subjects:

Procedures:

Situations:

(The exercise continues on the next page.)

(i) Evaluate the validity of the researcher's experimental and measured operational definitions:

(j) Evaluate the statistical conclusion validity of the results.

(k) From this experiment, how much confidence would you have that high-violence films produce greater levels of aggressive behavior in children than low-violence films?

None   0   1   2   3   4   5   6   7   A Great Deal

ANSWERS TO FILL-IN AND MULTIPLE CHOICE QUESTIONS

Fill-in

1. quality (429)
2. internal (430)
3. pact of ignorance (433)
4. statistical-conclusion (434)
5. effect size (435)
6. external (435)
7. subject (437)
8. operational (437)
9. aggregation (440)
10. measures (441)
11. multivariate (441)
12. MANOVA (442)
13. unobtrusive (443)
14. field (444)
15. naturalistic observation (445)
16. procedures (446)
17. hypothesis (448)

Multiple choice

1. a (432)
2. b (434)
3. b (435)
4. d (435)
5. a (437)
6. c (438)
7. d (439)
8. d (440)
9. b (441)
10. a (441)
11. c (443)
12. d (444)
13. c (445)
14. b (447)
15. d (448)
16. a (448)

SUGGESTED READINGS

Tan, A. S. (1986). Social learning of aggression from television. In J. Bryant & D. Zillmann (Eds.), *Perspectives on media effects* (pp. 41-55). Hillsdale, NJ: Lawrence Erlbaum.

16 CHAPTER SIXTEEN
Writing the Research Report

Chapter Outline

√√ CHAPTER OBJECTIVES: KEY CONCEPTS

Listed below are questions that test the major concepts you should know from Chapter 16. After reading the chapter, you should be able to answer each of the questions below. If not, go back to the book and read the appropriate sections again before continuing on in the Study Guide.

---

1.   What is the primary purpose of a <u>research report</u>? (454)

2.   What is meant by a <u>scientific writing style</u>? (454)

3.   What kinds of <u>biased language</u> need to be avoided? (455)

4.   What <u>format</u> is used for a research paper? (456)

5.   What is important for a <u>title</u>? (457)

6.   What are the basic requirements for the <u>Abstract</u>? (457)

7.   What is the purpose of the <u>Introduction</u>? (458)

8.   What information goes in the <u>Method</u> section? (459)

9.   What customary <u>subsections</u> are found in the Method section? (459)

10.   What is found in the <u>Results</u> section? (461)

11.   What is the purpose of the <u>Discussion</u>? (462)

12.   What is found in the list of <u>References</u>? (464)

13.   What was tested in the <u>sample journal article</u> by Borsari & Carey? (465)

154   Do you understand the <u>procedural details</u> for preparing your report? (478)

15.   What kinds of <u>common errors</u> can detract from a report? (483)

√ QUESTIONS FOR REVIEW AND STUDY

KEY TERMS: *define each term using your own words*

Research report (454):

Scientific writing style (454):

Title (457):

Abstract (457):

Introduction (458):

Method (459):

Results (461):

Discussion (462):

References (464):

Running head (478):

Page header (478):

√ QUESTIONS FOR REVIEW AND STUDY

FILL INS: *fill in the blanks with the right word or phrase*

1. Research reports are written in a _____ writing style that is highly structured and more concise than other kinds of writing.

2. The American Psychological Association and other journal publishers are committed to encouraging language free of _____ and _____ bias.

3. Psychological reports are expected to follow the format that is presented in detail in the _____ manual of the American Psychological Association.

4. The title of a research report should be _____ .

5. The _____ is a summary of the research report.

6. The abstract of a research report is particularly important because it will appear in publications such as Psychological _____ and computer resources like _____ .

7. The Abstract is probably the most frequently _____ portion of any article.

8. The _____ should be explicitly stated in the Introduction of the research report.

9. The introduction to your research report should leave readers prepared for the _____ section.

10. The information provided in the Participants subsection of the Method section should allow the reader to assess the _____ of your results.

11. What you did and how you did it should go in the _____ subsection of the Method section.

12. The Procedure subsection of the Method section should explain the procedures you used for controlling _____ variables.

13. The Results section of a report should tell readers what _____ procedures you used and what you found.

14. Estimates of effect _____ are strongly recommended in the *APA Publication Manual*.

15. We interpret the effects of statistical tests in the _____ section.

16. Any articles or books mentioned in a research report should be listed in the _____ section.

17. The _____ , which is the first few words of your title, appears on every page of your manuscript.

Correct answers are located at the end of the chapter, but do not look at them until you have completed the test.

√ QUESTIONS FOR REVIEW AND STUDY

MULTIPLE CHOICE: *circle the best answer to each question*

1. A well-written research report includes all of the following except
   _____ .
   a. information for replicating the research
   b. life experiences and personal opinions
   c. precise, parsimonious, and unbiased language
   d. scientific findings

2. A good way to avoid sexist language is _____ .
   a. to pluralize sentences
   b. to use the construction s/he instead of he
   c. to use the word mankind in place of man
   d. to avoid personal pronouns

3. Why do we use the American Psychological Association format for writing reports?
   a. It cuts down on the number of articles published.
   b. It is easier to type than other report formats.
   c. It is more formal and makes the document more scientific.
   d. It makes the job of reporting easier for writers and readers.

4. Which of the following is the most descriptive title?
   a. A Psychology Experiment Testing Violent and Nonviolent Films
   b. Fight Night at the Films: A Critical Test
   c. The Effects of Film Violence on Children's Aggressive Behavior
   d. Some Effects of Movies on Children

5. Which of the following is the most frequently read portion of a research article?
   a. Abstract
   b. Results
   c. Introduction
   d. Tables and Graphs

302

6. In the Introduction, you should do all of the following except _____ .
    a. state your hypothesis or hypotheses explicitly
    b. cite all the past studies that relate to your general topic area
    c. prepare readers for what follows in the report
    d. include a concise review of the literature that led to your hypothesis

7. Participants and Apparatus are subsections of the _____ section.
    a. Materials
    b. Results
    c. Experiment
    d. Method

8. Which of the following should not be included in the Results section?
    a. critical values from statistical tables
    b. significance level
    c. measure(s) of variability
    d. obtained statistical values

9. When typing a research report, which of the following shows the correct way to present your statistical values?
    a. $F(1,30) = 6.65, p < .05$
    b. $\underline{F}(1,30) = 6.65, \underline{p} < .05$
    c. $F = 6.65, df = 1$ and $30, p < .05$
    d. $F(p < .05) = 6.65 (1,30)$

10. Sources of confounding or other problems in an experiment would be explained in the _____ section.
    a. Introduction
    b. Results
    c. Discussion
    d. Method

11. Which of the following results best describes Borsari & Carey's findings in the sample journal article?
    a. Women reported drinking less than men at baseline, but men's drinking decreased more after the intervention.
    b. The brief intervention reduced drinking behavior and RAPI scores.
    c. The group receiving the brief intervention reported less drinking at the 6-week follow-up.
    d. The only significant influence on decreasing drinking behaviors was the gender of the subject.

12. When typing a book reference for a research report, only the _____ is italicized.
   a. name of the author or authors
   b. title of the book
   c. volume number
   d. publisher's city

13. Which of the following would not be expected to appear on the title page of a research report?
   a. the complete title of the report
   b. names of the author or authors
   c. the university or business affiliation of the author(s)
   d. the class for which you are writing the paper

14. A running head is _____ .
   a. a shortened title printed above the pages to help readers identify the article
   b. a header that includes the name and affiliation of the author or authors
   c. a page header that helps the publisher keep the pages together
   d. a summary (<120 words) of the report that goes near the top of page 2

15. A research report would include an Appendix only if _____.
   a. the reviewers felt that the material justified the extra journal page or pages
   b. the material was designed by the author(s) for this study and cannot be obtained elsewhere
   c. the material is necessary for the reader but would be distracting if presented in the text
   d. different procedures were used in different portions of the experiment

16. When typing a research report, always begin the _____ section on a new page.
   a. Method
   b. Results
   c. Discussion
   d. References

Correct answers are located at the end of the chapter, but do not look at them until you have completed the test.

√ QUESTIONS FOR REVIEW AND STUDY

SHORT ESSAY: use the information in the chapter to answer the following questions

1. What are the major goals of a research report?

2. What is meant by a scientific writing style?

3.   What information goes into the Introduction?

4.   What information goes into the Method section?

5.   What information goes into the Results section?

6.   What information goes into the Discussion?

√ EXERCISES AND APPLICATIONS

1. Return to the confounded experiment on film violence from the previous chapter.

    (a) Use your work on the exercise to write a brief Method section. When you describe the experiment, be sure to incorporate any changes you suggested in part f (changes in procedures) and in part i (changes in the operational definitions). Use the four subsection heads that are provided below: Participants, Materials, Procedure, and Design.

Participants

Materials

Procedure

(The exercise continues on the next page.)

(b) Now, construct a brief Results section describing the results of the 2 X 2 ANOVA given in the exercise. Plan it in the following way: Report all three statistical values in the text, and include your effect size estimates. Report the condition means for the main effects in the text, but refer readers to a table (Table 1) for the group means for the interaction and the post hoc results.

(The exercise continues on the next page.)

(c) Assume the experiment was actually conducted using your new and improved procedures, rather than the original procedures described in the confounded experiment. Write a first draft of a short Discussion section. Begin by stating the major findings (in words). Then, follow the Discussion section guidelines in Chapter 16 of your text. Be sure to answer the following questions: "Was your hypothesis supported?" "How do the findings fit in with prior research in the area?" "What are the implications of the research?" Can you generalize from the findings?" (Keep in mind that only one and a half workbook pages are provided for you, and you must keep to that limit.)

To write the discussion, you may assume the following:
  (1) From your review of past research, you predicted each of the three significant effects. (You had three hypotheses; each was supported.)
  (2) The results from your experiment are consistent with findings from prior research (in fact, they are!). For example, they are consistent with conclusions from the Tan (1986) review chapter from the Suggested Readings section, so you may use that reference in your Discussion.

(Continue the Discussion on the next page.)